The Complete Book of
Sketching

First published in Great Britain in 2003 by Cassell Illustrated,
a division of Octopus Publishing Group Limited

This edition published 2003 by Chancellor Press, an imprint of Bounty Books,
a division of Octopus Publishing Group Limited,
2-4 Heron Quays, London E14 4JP

A CIP catalogue record for this book is available from the British Library.

Much of the material in this book has been previously published
in John Hamilton's *Sketching with a Pencil* (1989) and *Sketching at Home* (1991);
Sharon Finmark's *Sketching Indoors* (1999); John Marsh's *Sketching Landscapes* (1998)
and *Sketching Street Scenes* (1999); Robert Norrington's *Sketching Harbours and Boats* (1999)

ISBN 0 7537 0778 0

Printed in China by Midas Printing International Ltd.

The Complete Book of
Sketching

John Hamilton • Sharon Finmark • John Marsh • Robert Norrington

CHANCELLOR PRESS

Contents

Part 1
The Bare Essentials

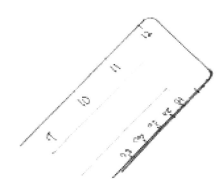

The Bare Essentials

So many people seem to give up drawing almost before they have begun. This is usually because they choose a subject which is too difficult, and not surprisingly they are disheartened by the result. **We** are not going to fall into that trap.

Having said that, let's begin.

Firstly, what equipment should you have?

For your SKETCH BOOK, choose one with a strong cardboard back and some form of spiral binding. A glued binding tends to fall apart with use, and particularly so if it gets wet. As for size, I use an A4 (the same size as this book), but with experience you will find the size that suits you. Stick to that size. A smooth white paper can be found at your art shop, and it will be adequate for your early work. Always include a large BULLDOG clip to stop the paper blowing in the wind, and include a clear plastic 12 inch RULER.

Your PENCILS should be good quality, and I suggest HB, 2B, 4B and 6B. Pencils are graded from 6H which is very hard and is used mostly by draughtsmen, through to 6B which is soft and very black. HB is in the middle. You can always add to your collection at any time, but I want to start you off with the minimum of equipment so as not to confuse you.

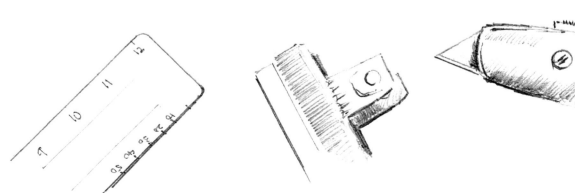

You must include a very sharp KNIFE. A Stanley type is ideal, and a pencil sharpener can be included, although it does not give you a long enough point for everything you will want to do. Put a strip of fine sandpaper in your bag. It will be invaluable for sharpening up the point of your pencils.

Include a good RUBBER. The best kind will be very soft and bungy, and large enough not to become lost.

Finally we come to the all-important question of a comfortable STOOL. There are all kinds and sizes on the market, but I went to a fishing tackle shop and found an ideal model. It is light, and has a strap which enables you to carry it from the shoulder and thus have both hands free. However the best thing about it is that it has a waterproof bag attached to the side of the stool, and it carries all my equipment.

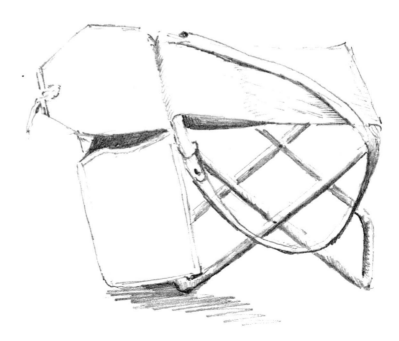

First Strokes

Before you start drawing, I am going to suggest that you use the last page of your sketch book or any spare sheet of paper to try out your pencils and discover the difference between HB and 6B. Look at the shading I have done opposite and do the same. Relax your wrist, practise starting with quite firm pressure and then gradually slacken off. You will find the secret is a supple wrist.

Try laying your ruler on the page and shading up to it.

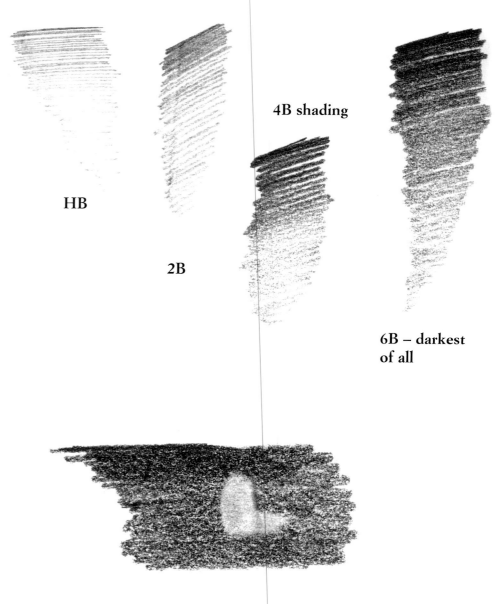

4B shading

HB

2B

6B

4B

6B – darkest of all

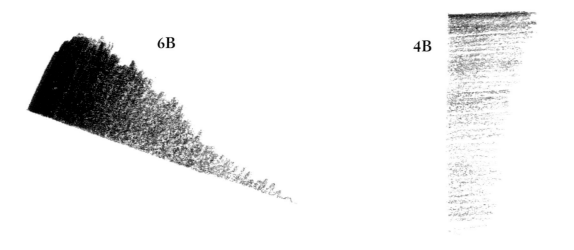

Finally use your rubber, but beware! Clean the rubber on a spare piece of paper after each use. In this way it won't make smudges on your work.

Have fun, and keep practising. The golden rule is a light touch and a supple wrist. See how dark you can make your shading, then release the pressure gradually to let it become lighter and lighter until it is hardly visible.

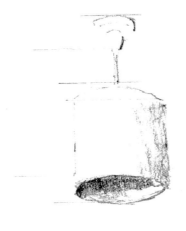

4B **2B**

Sketching at Home

The advantage of sketching in the home is that everything you want is at hand. Even if you have only thirty minutes to spare there is something you can do.

I don't want to impose anything on you, but remember that you are only just beginning. It is frustrating to choose a subject which is beyond you and make a mess of it. 'Oh I can't draw,' you'll say, but it isn't true. The problem is that you crossed over into the fast lane after the first driving lesson.

Why not try something simple, like a lamp shade or perhaps a part of a wooden chair? Not the whole chair, just a corner of the back of the chair. I have done the same lamp shade with different shading. Start by sketching in the lamp very lightly, so corrections are easy, and don't be afraid to use your rubber.

I went round the house drawing different lights and experimenting with shading. The result was that I became flexible and relaxed, beginning to see subjects for a sketch which I had never thought suitable.

There's a useful saying about shading: 'If in doubt, leave it out.'

Here is a little exercise with still life. Place the objects on a table and shine a light from one side. Don't move them, but walk round the table to find the most attractive composition. Decide how dark you want your finished work to be. My cube became a box and was more attractive with a lighter shade. In this exercise I used 2B and 4B pencils.

When you start a sketch like this use the lightest of touch to draw in the outlines. I used a 2B pencil with a **very** sharp point. My large soft rubber with a straight edge was invaluable. This kind of drawing is not always easy, and if it doesn't appeal to you – don't push it, but stick to subjects in which you feel confident.

Remember – keep your pencils sharp. I had a strip of sandpaper by me and after making a long point with my knife, I used the sandpaper to keep the point sharp.

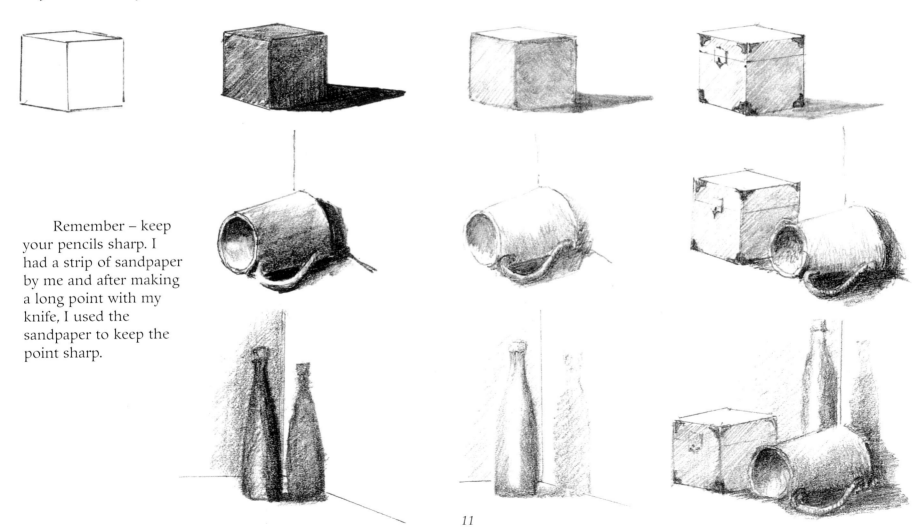

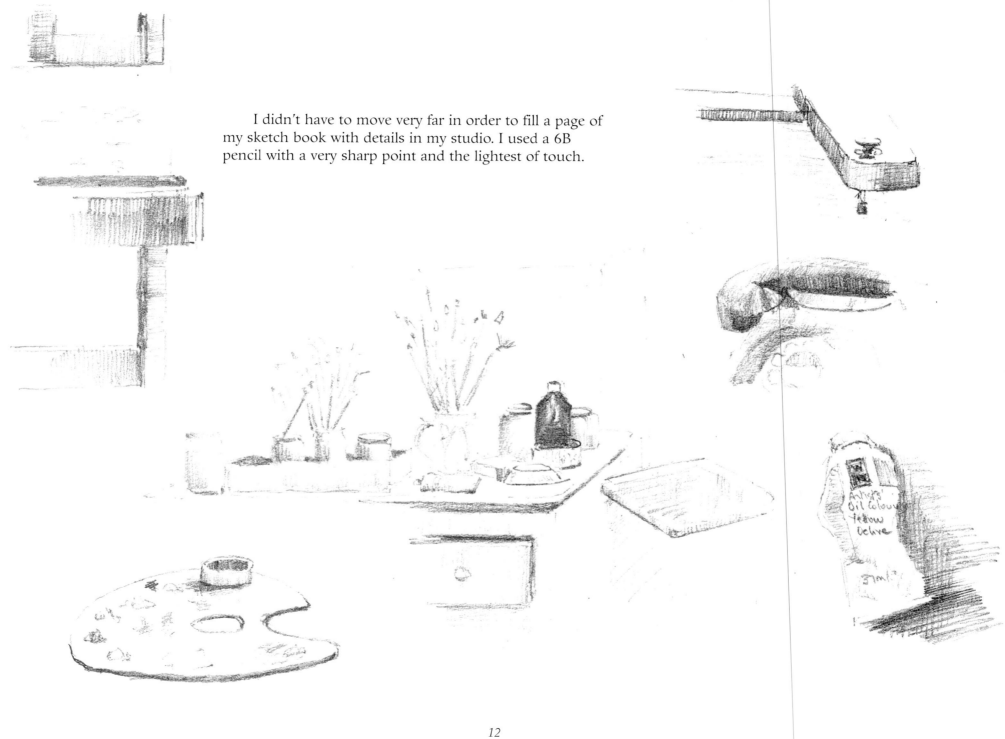

I didn't have to move very far in order to fill a page of
my sketch book with details in my studio. I used a 6B
pencil with a very sharp point and the lightest of touch.

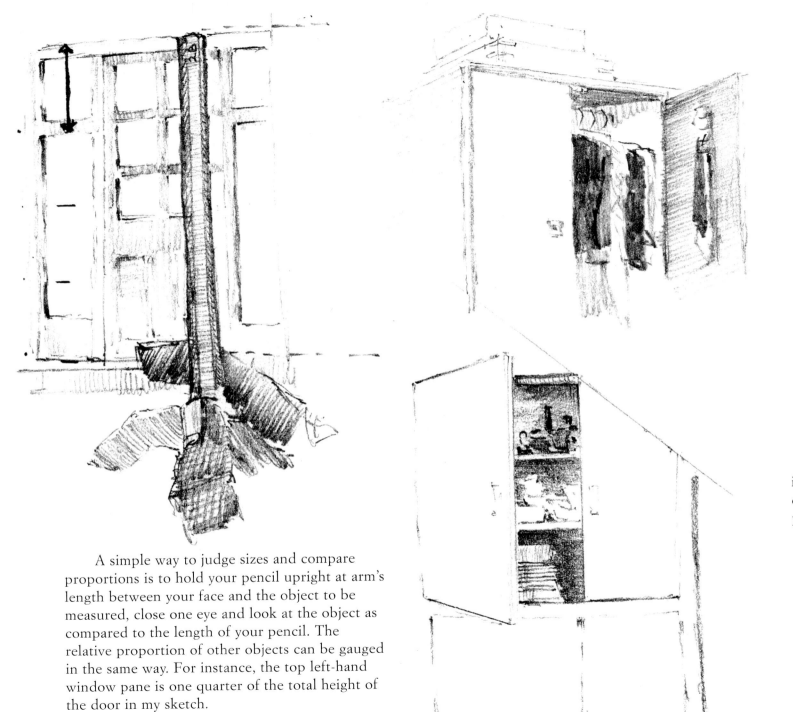

Doors of all kinds are interesting and useful subjects for a drawing. (They are also good for practising perspective. Read on!)

A simple way to judge sizes and compare proportions is to hold your pencil upright at arm's length between your face and the object to be measured, close one eye and look at the object as compared to the length of your pencil. The relative proportion of other objects can be gauged in the same way. For instance, the top left-hand window pane is one quarter of the total height of the door in my sketch.

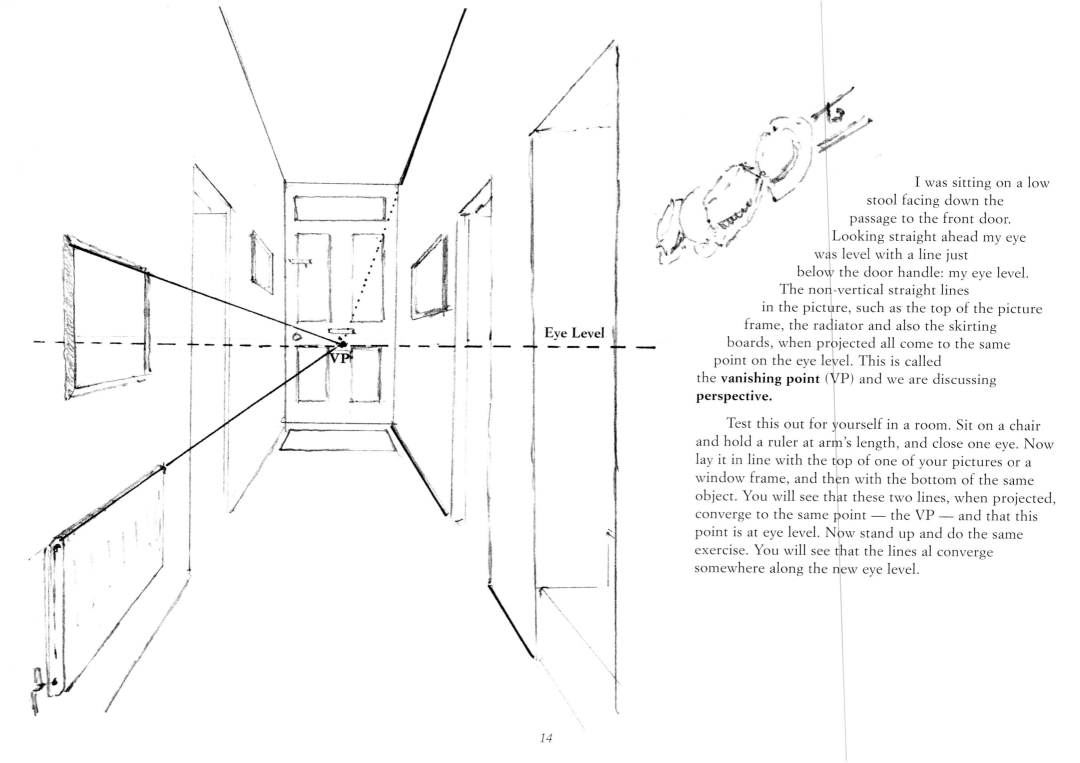

Eye Level

VP

I was sitting on a low stool facing down the passage to the front door. Looking straight ahead my eye was level with a line just below the door handle: my eye level. The non-vertical straight lines in the picture, such as the top of the picture frame, the radiator and also the skirting boards, when projected all come to the same point on the eye level. This is called the **vanishing point** (VP) and we are discussing **perspective.**

Test this out for yourself in a room. Sit on a chair and hold a ruler at arm's length, and close one eye. Now lay it in line with the top of one of your pictures or a window frame, and then with the bottom of the same object. You will see that these two lines, when projected, converge to the same point — the VP — and that this point is at eye level. Now stand up and do the same exercise. You will see that the lines al converge somewhere along the new eye level.

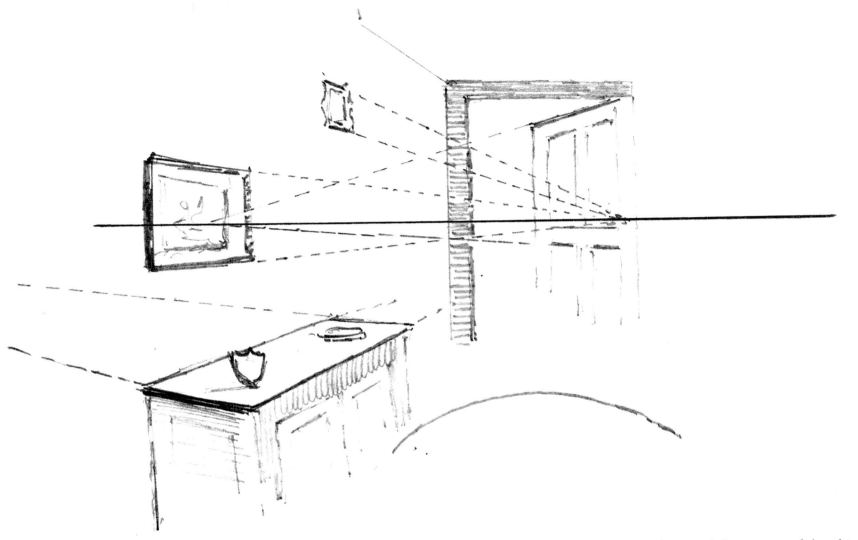

I sat at a table looking towards the door into the kitchen, and drew some of the objects around me. The dark horizontal line shows my eye level. The pictures on the wall to the left all lead my eye to a VP straight ahead. The partly open door led off to a VP to the left, but again somewhere on the eye level. The top of the cabinet led off to a VP a long way to the left, but again at eye level.

Try to do this yourself. Sit not exactly in the centre of a room, facing a wall. Look straight ahead and make a mental note of the line of your eye level. Very faintly draw in this line and make a sketch of the scene before you, being sure to include pictures and perhaps a window on the left or right. Now stop drawing and by laying your ruler along the top and bottom of any pictures or windows you have drawn, see if the lines converge to a VP. Don't be disheartened if they don't; in time perspective will become second nature.

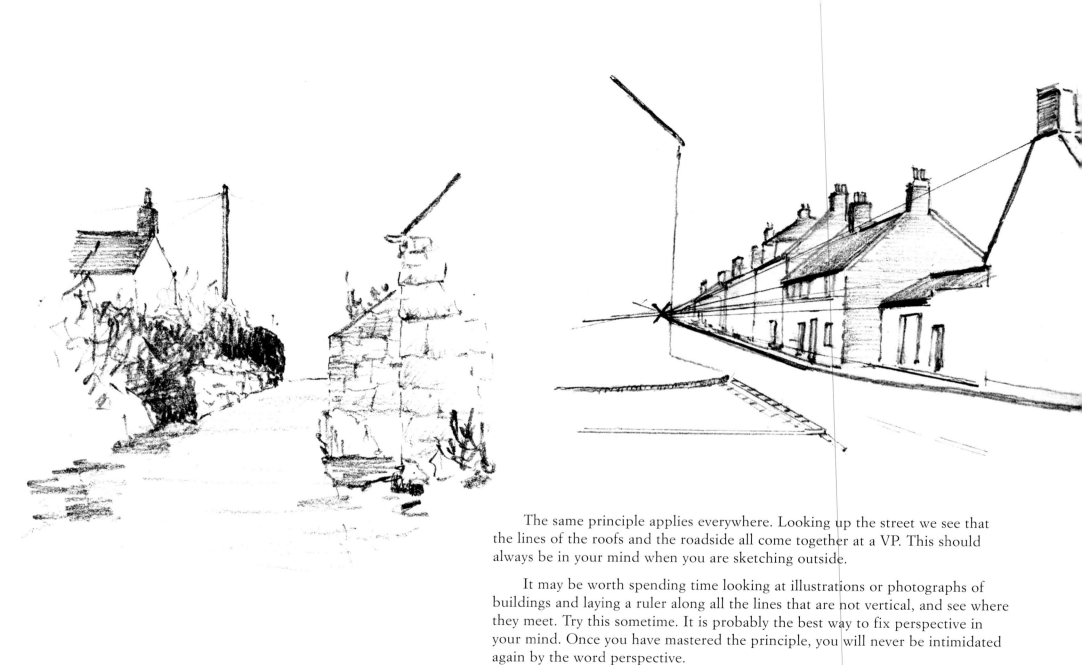

The same principle applies everywhere. Looking up the street we see that the lines of the roofs and the roadside all come together at a VP. This should always be in your mind when you are sketching outside.

It may be worth spending time looking at illustrations or photographs of buildings and laying a ruler along all the lines that are not vertical, and see where they meet. Try this sometime. It is probably the best way to fix perspective in your mind. Once you have mastered the principle, you will never be intimidated again by the word perspective.

I don't want to spend too much time on perspective, important though it is, and we will return to it later. By now I hope you will have found that there is a wealth of possible subjects for a sketch in the house. Keep to the principle of using a really light touch to start with and when you are satisfied with the main structure, bring it all to life with shading. The spoons are a case in point. I used a 2B pencil for a faint outline, but now we have a feeling that they are standing out from the wall.

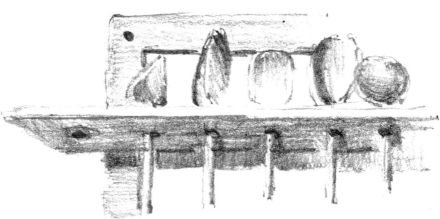

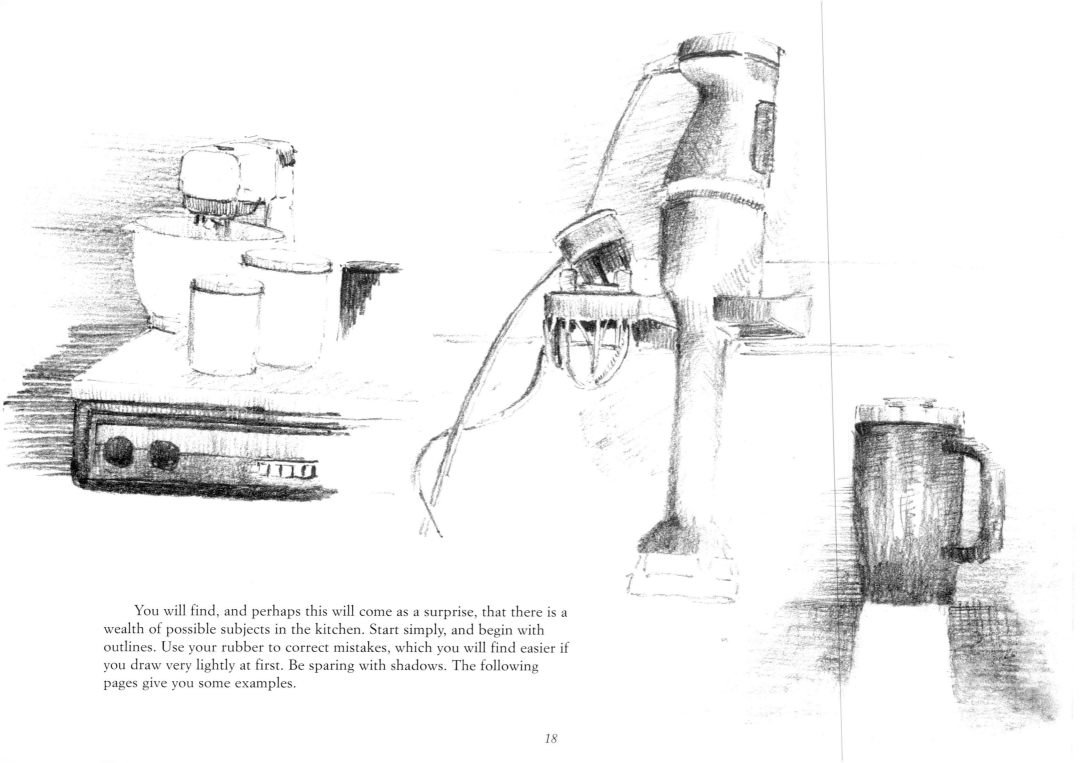

You will find, and perhaps this will come as a surprise, that there is a wealth of possible subjects in the kitchen. Start simply, and begin with outlines. Use your rubber to correct mistakes, which you will find easier if you draw very lightly at first. Be sparing with shadows. The following pages give you some examples.

Sitting in the kitchen for an hour produces these little sketches.

From where you happen to be sitting you will find all kinds of objects that are interesting to draw. Just sketch away with a light touch using an HB or 2B pencil. Contrary to what many people think, I never have any hesitation in using my rubber, but avoid taking out heavy shading or you will smudge your work. — So, start off lightly and satisfy yourself that your outline is correct before doing any heavy shading. If you must remove some dark pencil work, for instance, when putting in highlights, clean your rubber after each stroke.

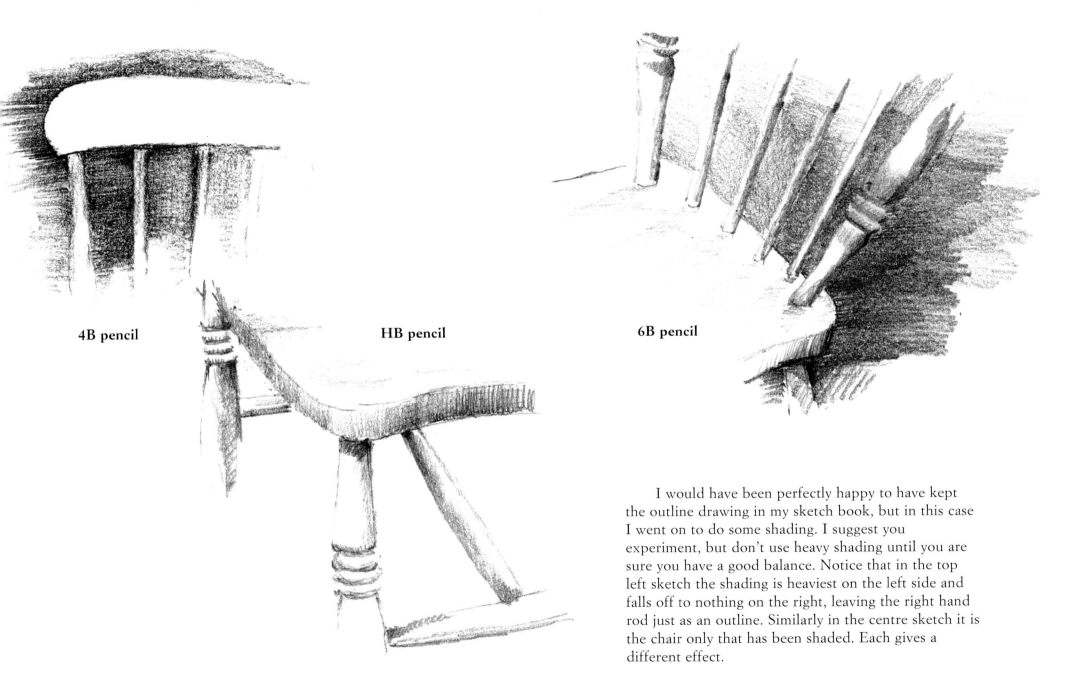

4B pencil

HB pencil

6B pencil

I would have been perfectly happy to have kept the outline drawing in my sketch book, but in this case I went on to do some shading. I suggest you experiment, but don't use heavy shading until you are sure you have a good balance. Notice that in the top left sketch the shading is heaviest on the left side and falls off to nothing on the right, leaving the right hand rod just as an outline. Similarly in the centre sketch it is the chair only that has been shaded. Each gives a different effect.

Still-life still has to live! Whether it is a collection of bottles or a bowl of fruit, it is either alive or it is flat. So how do we go about tackling a bowl of assorted fruits?

I suggest that you spend a moment or two composing the fruit, and noticing how the light falls on the surfaces. Try not to complicate the subject, which is already quite challenging.

Personally, I spend quite a long time endeavouring to draw the outline accurately and to scale. This I do with a very light touch, using an HB or a 2B pencil, and my rubber.

Have you ever thought of looking at what you have done through a mirror? It is an excellent way to check on your ability in handling shapes and symmetry. Why not find a hand mirror now and look at what you have done. It is surprising how errors show up if you reverse the image.

Here is the second stage in my still-life drawing. I have begun to put in the deeper shadows, but have not concentrated on any one piece of fruit. I am endeavouring to keep a balance. The bowl is formed of elaborate and highly coloured tracery, but you will see that I don't want it to dominate.

This is the last stage. It is always a problem to know when to stop, and if there is any advice I can give, it would be to stop too early rather than too late. There is a temptation to fiddle with a pencil and this can often spoil your picture. Here, the bowl is almost as detailed as the fruit. Any more detail on the bowl would bring the eye down from the fruit to concentrate on the bowl — and the subject of the sketch would be lost.

I think I might agree with you if you said I had gone too far already.

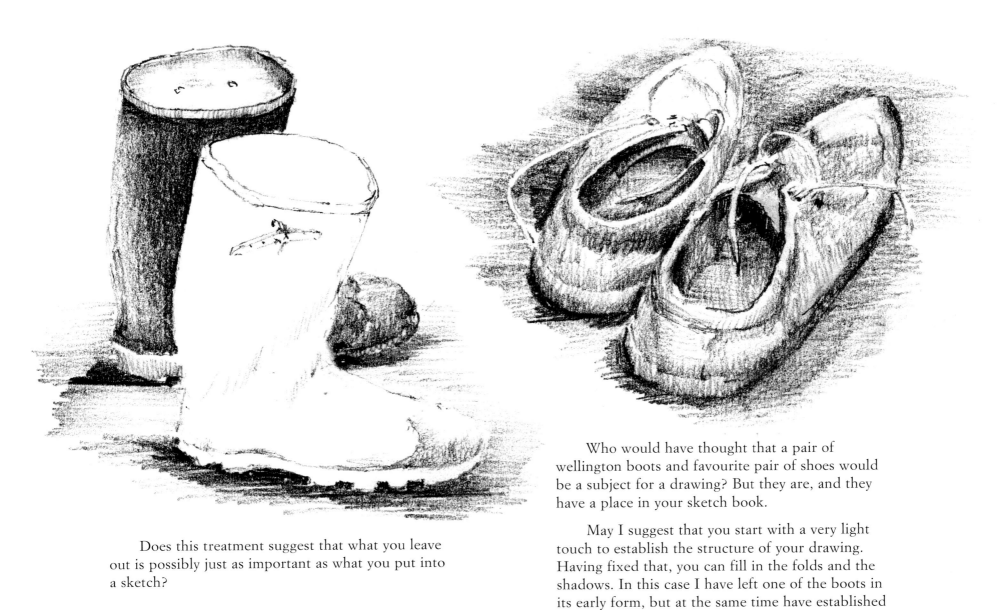

Does this treatment suggest that what you leave out is possibly just as important as what you put into a sketch?

Who would have thought that a pair of wellington boots and favourite pair of shoes would be a subject for a drawing? But they are, and they have a place in your sketch book.

May I suggest that you start with a very light touch to establish the structure of your drawing. Having fixed that, you can fill in the folds and the shadows. In this case I have left one of the boots in its early form, but at the same time have established its position on the ground with deep 4B shading.

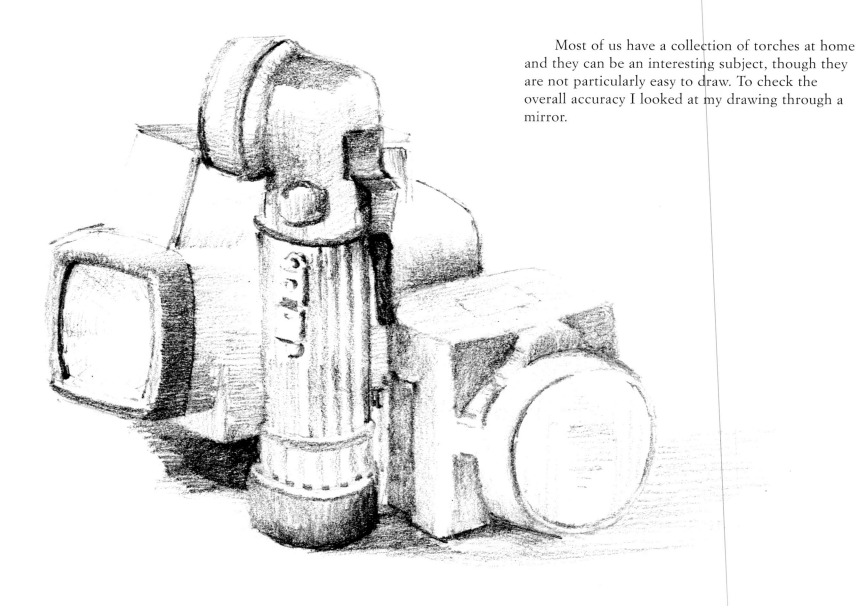

Most of us have a collection of torches at home and they can be an interesting subject, though they are not particularly easy to draw. To check the overall accuracy I looked at my drawing through a mirror.

Here is a suggestion for a part of the keyboard of a typewriter. First an outline drawing and a little shading.

Now we've got it just about right. Note what I have left out.

Now we've spoiled it by doing too much!

Notice how this sketch has been built up.

I started with very faint outlines which established the structure of the instrument and the telephone directory beneath it (but I had to make good use of my rubber before I got it right!). All this was with a 2B pencil. Shading began with the darkest shadows with a 4B, but I have left one side unshaded to show you how it developed. Think about the effectiveness of the heavy shading (and the direction of the lines of the pencil) against the outline of the book.

Finally, don't forget to practise your shading exercises. They will help you to achieve a supple wrist and lightness of touch.

If you want to try your hand at a table lamp illuminating a room, remember that the area surrounding the light must be darker than the light source. In the sketches on this and the following page I have chosen the light as the focal point of the drawing with the shadows giving strength to the surrounding area. Once again it is important to stress that a light touch at the start with an HB pencil will help you to design the layout.

Notice how the light stands out against the darker background.

Here is a different treatment. I did the outline drawing but attempted to show that the light was on.

There was an attractive round window in the wall of a friend's sitting room. I sketched it lightly and then shaded it but I liked the composition of the whole corner of that room so did another sketch including the lamp, table and chair – all in outline.

As the sketch developed I did exactly the reverse. I left the window almost totally unshaded and made the round table the central part of the drawing. It was a light and airy room with lots of windows; I tried to convey that by leaving the back of the arm chair unshaded and strengthening the shadow from the lamp.

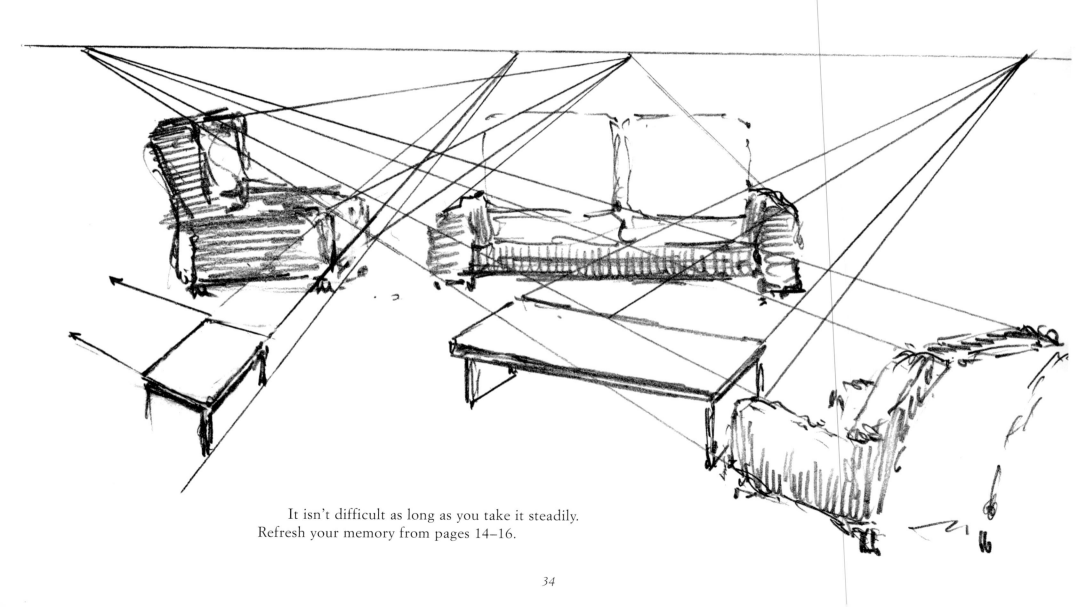

It isn't difficult as long as you take it steadily.
Refresh your memory from pages 14–16.

Look at these two pages. The cubes represent some of the furniture on the opposite page which is pointing in different directions. Before you go any further why not arrange some of the pieces in your room so that they are not all parallel. Hold your ruler or your sketch book at arm's length and look along the lines to discover how many vanishing points there are.

VP   **VP**   **VP**   **Eye level**   **VP**

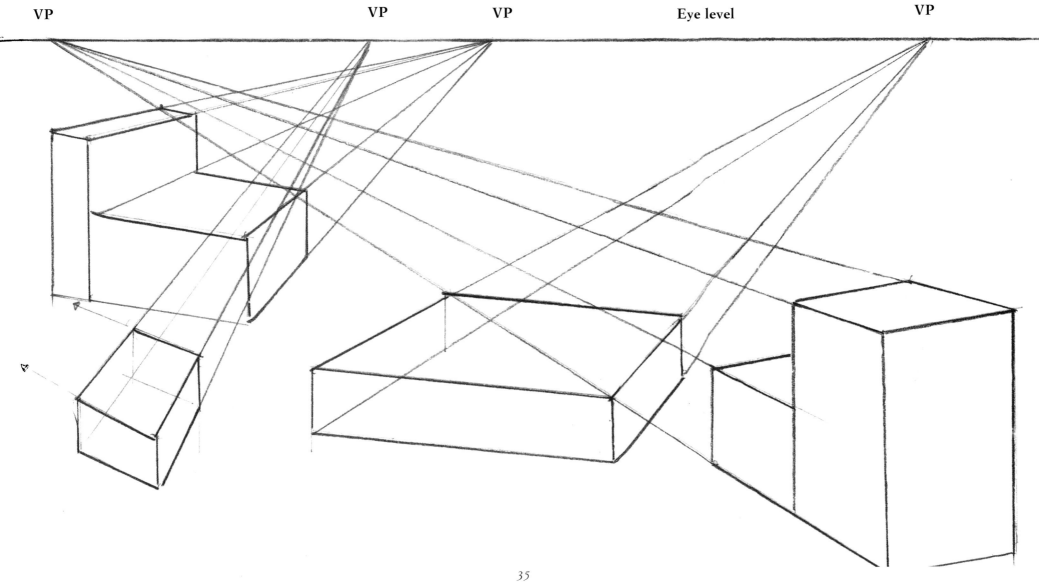

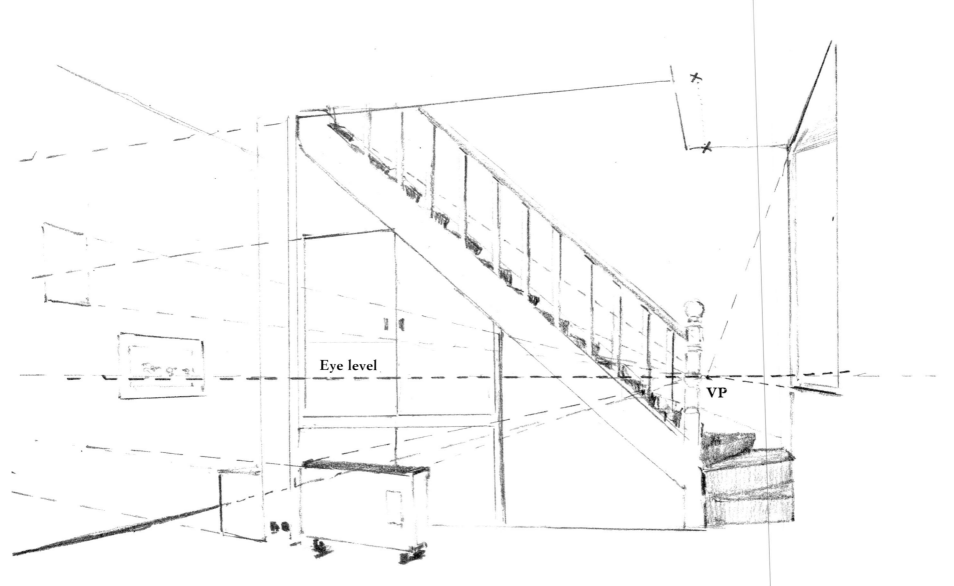

Eye level

VP

Stairs are intriguing subjects, whether drawn form above or below, and pose their own problems of perspective. In the earlier discussion of perspective, I said that there could be more than one vanishing point: here is an example. I was sitting on a chair and my eye level was as shown. However, if you look to the left you will see that the cupboard door, the electric heater and the ceiling above the stairs all project naturally towards the left to a VP along the eye level, but a long way beyond the drawing. The rest of the drawing leads you down to the central VP. Experiment with this, holding out a long ruler against non-vertical straight edges of items in the room. You will see how it all works out.

Here is the completed sketch. Lay a ruler along all the non-vertical lines and see whether you can find the vanishing points. Does my drawing reflect accurately what I have been saying?

Shading has played an important part. The first sketch which was completely flat established the position of the different angles in the room. When I began I used the small area between the Xs on the earlier sketch as my measuring scale. Holding my pencil upright at arm's length I measured that small piece of wall, then found that the handrail was five times as long, the top of the under-stair cupboard just slightly longer than my scale, and so on. The composition could have been improved by including a chair or a small table in the foreground but I have resisted doing this so as to make this a clear perspective exercise.

Sometimes a sketch will 'expand outwards' from a central theme. In this case I liked the flowered cushion on the chair and did an outline sketch, and then felt sufficiently confident to develop the drawing by including the chair, curtain and window. I didn't draw everything – I left out the carpet and only gave a suggestion of the tables.

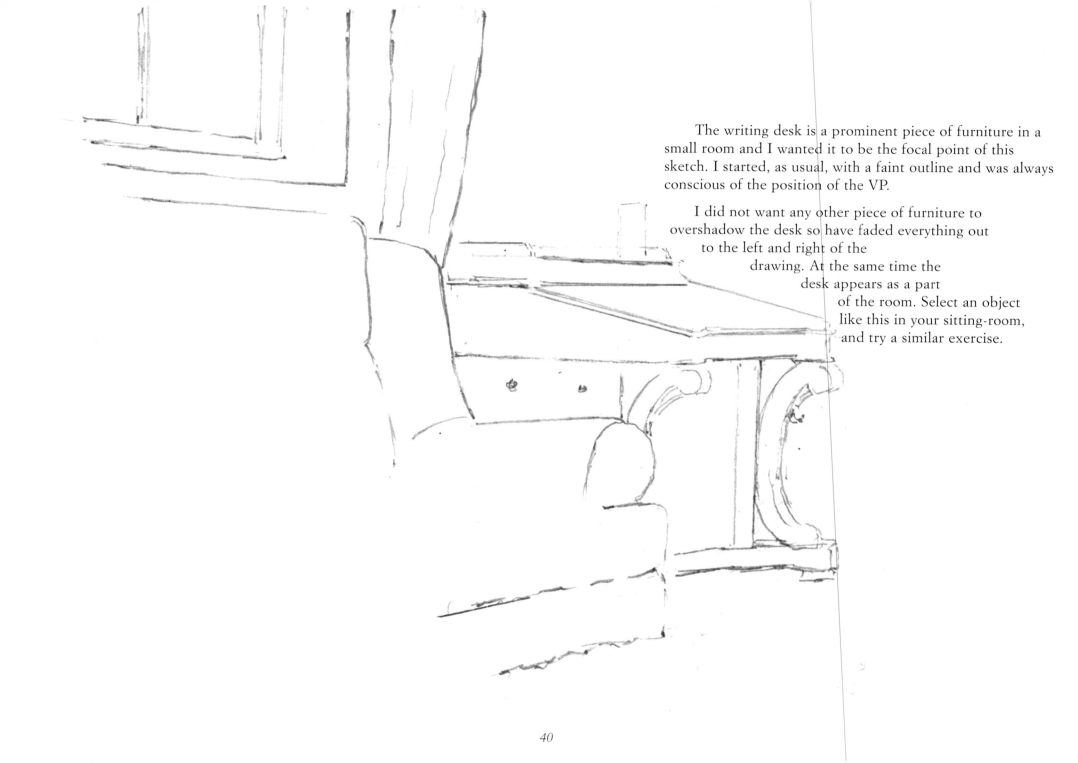

The writing desk is a prominent piece of furniture in a small room and I wanted it to be the focal point of this sketch. I started, as usual, with a faint outline and was always conscious of the position of the VP.

I did not want any other piece of furniture to overshadow the desk so have faded everything out to the left and right of the drawing. At the same time the desk appears as a part of the room. Select an object like this in your sitting-room, and try a similar exercise.

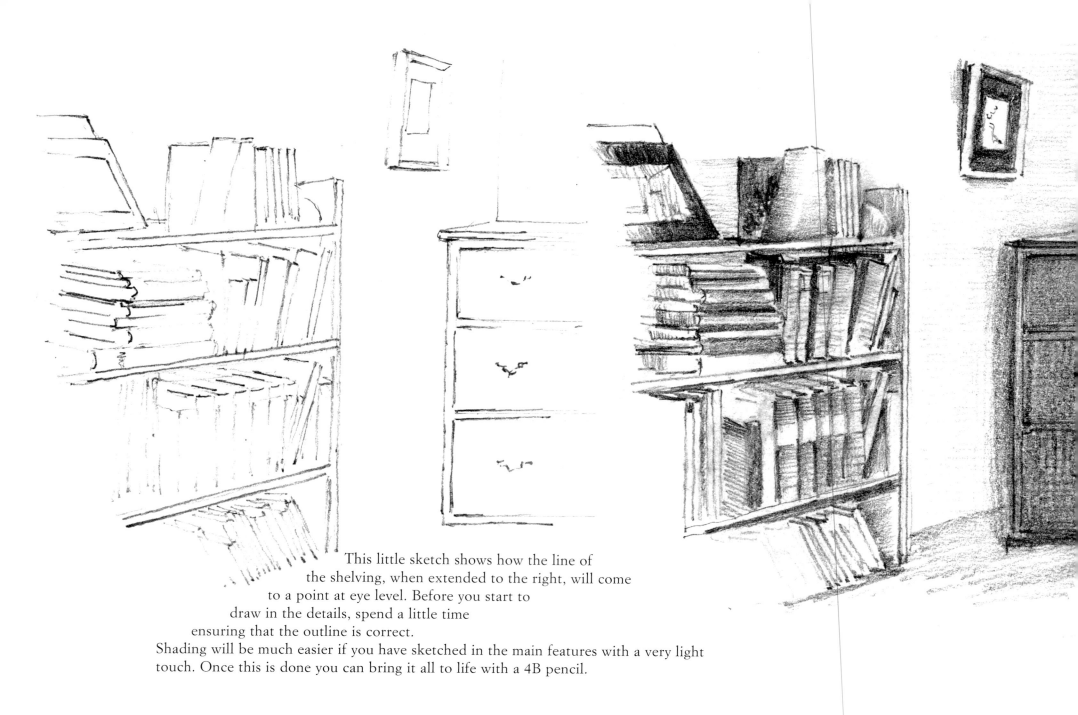

This little sketch shows how the line of
the shelving, when extended to the right, will come
to a point at eye level. Before you start to
draw in the details, spend a little time
ensuring that the outline is correct.
Shading will be much easier if you have sketched in the main features with a very light
touch. Once this is done you can bring it all to life with a 4B pencil.

Even the bathroom has possibilities and you will
be tackling a number of problems here. Sketch in
outline first and build up your shading later to make the
individual objects stand out.

43

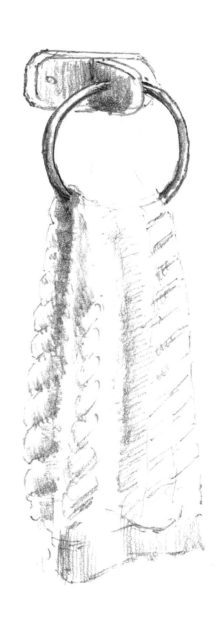

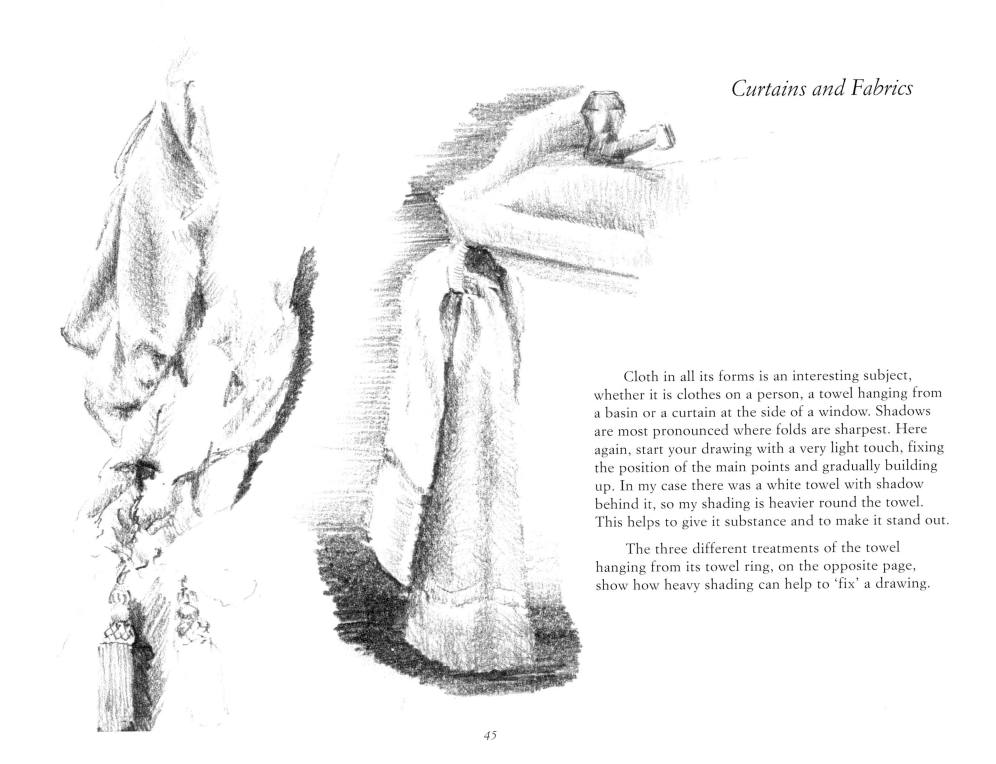

Curtains and Fabrics

Cloth in all its forms is an interesting subject, whether it is clothes on a person, a towel hanging from a basin or a curtain at the side of a window. Shadows are most pronounced where folds are sharpest. Here again, start your drawing with a very light touch, fixing the position of the main points and gradually building up. In my case there was a white towel with shadow behind it, so my shading is heavier round the towel. This helps to give it substance and to make it stand out.

The three different treatments of the towel hanging from its towel ring, on the opposite page, show how heavy shading can help to 'fix' a drawing.

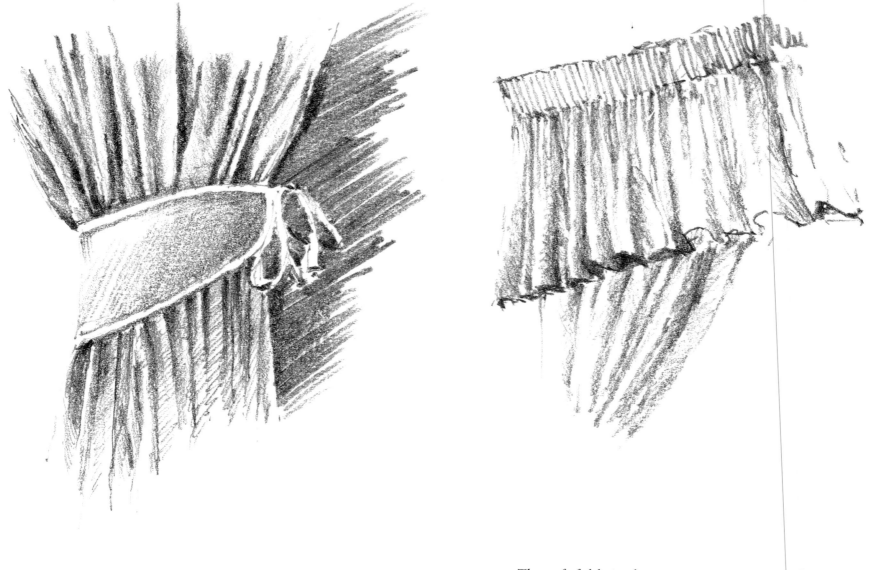

The soft folds in these curtains are captured here in simple light and shade. In the pelmet on the right the depths of the folds are generally shaded, while the forward curves of the material are left white — an effective representation of the real thing.

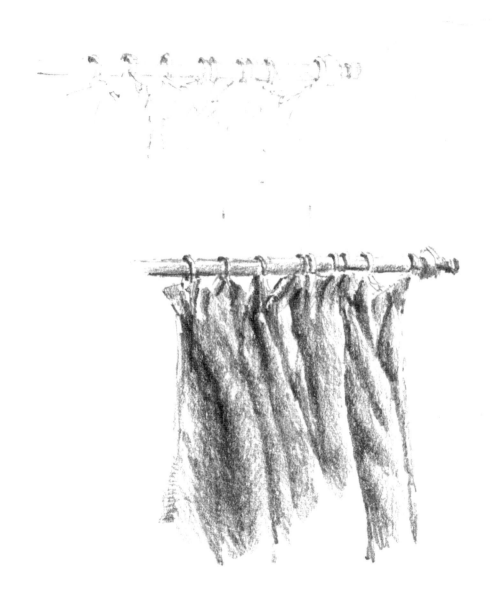

Spend half an hour drawing the curtains in your sitting-room. Don't worry about a 'finished' drawing, just draw the outline softly and practise shading. Fill the page of your book with details of the curtains and I think you will be surprised at how dramatically you can produce folds after a little practice.

I think most families have 'special people', and I
am sure that they have a place in our sketch book.

More special people, and they are not heavily shaded. In real life the teddy bear on the right is much darker than I have shaded him.

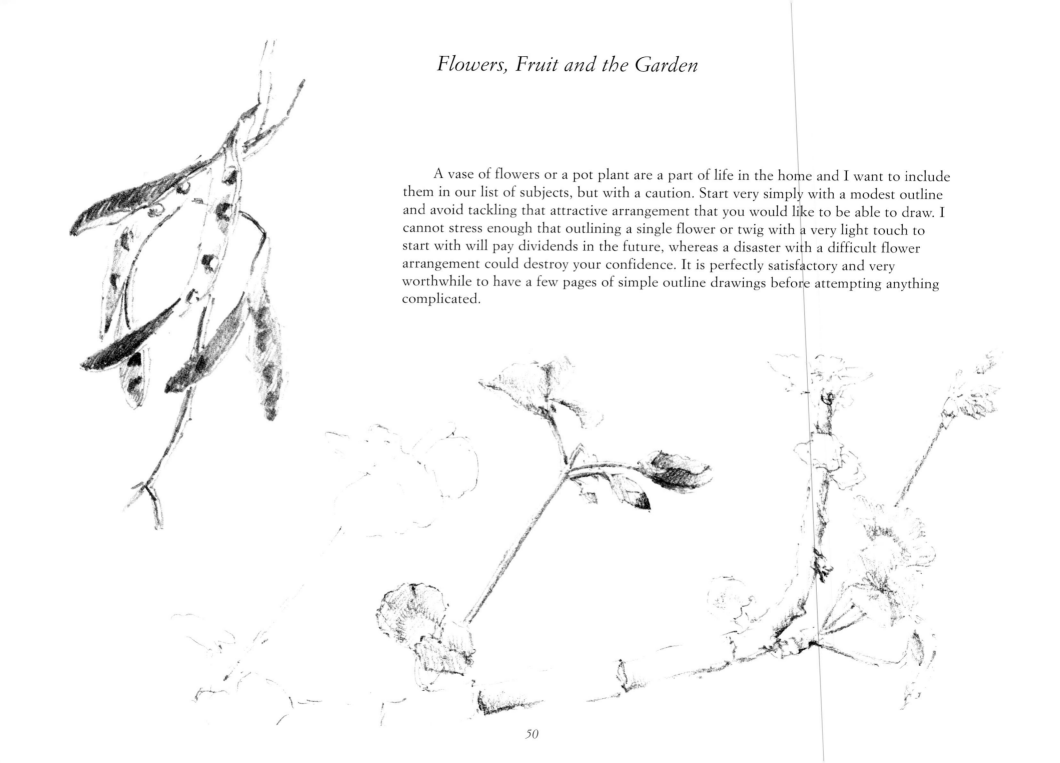

Flowers, Fruit and the Garden

A vase of flowers or a pot plant are a part of life in the home and I want to include them in our list of subjects, but with a caution. Start very simply with a modest outline and avoid tackling that attractive arrangement that you would like to be able to draw. I cannot stress enough that outlining a single flower or twig with a very light touch to start with will pay dividends in the future, whereas a disaster with a difficult flower arrangement could destroy your confidence. It is perfectly satisfactory and very worthwhile to have a few pages of simple outline drawings before attempting anything complicated.

I sketched the outline of this cyclamen, trying to be accurate. It was a light pink flower against a darker background and I decided to use a 4B pencil to give some depth to this. Notice that I have graded my shading. I used a rubber to pick out the highlights — cleaning it after each stroke.

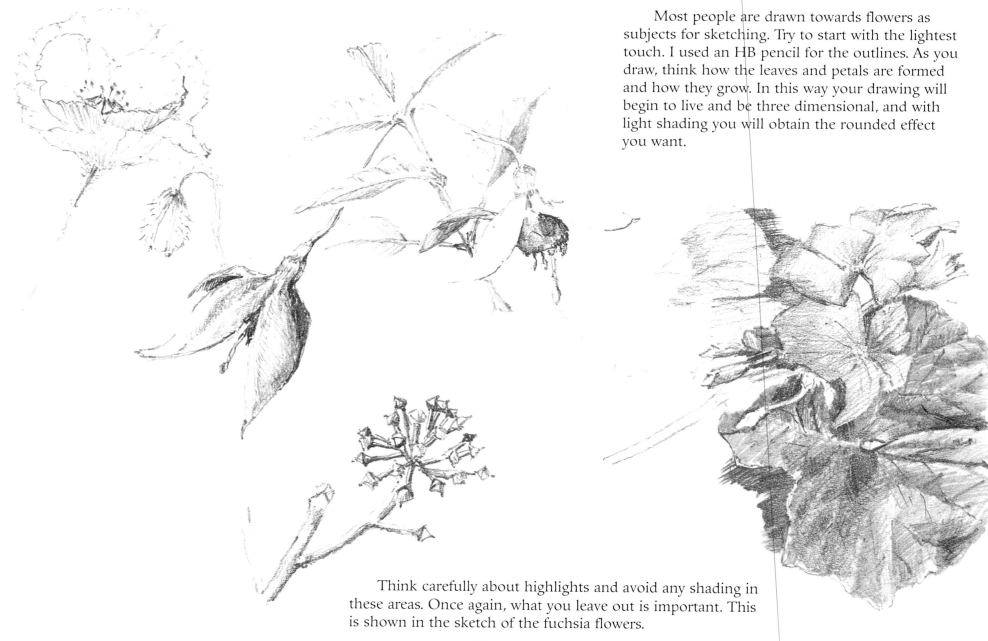

Most people are drawn towards flowers as subjects for sketching. Try to start with the lightest touch. I used an HB pencil for the outlines. As you draw, think how the leaves and petals are formed and how they grow. In this way your drawing will begin to live and be three dimensional, and with light shading you will obtain the rounded effect you want.

Think carefully about highlights and avoid any shading in these areas. Once again, what you leave out is important. This is shown in the sketch of the fuchsia flowers.

Be sure to draw a very light outline of each leaf and flower before you attempt to go on to heavier shading.

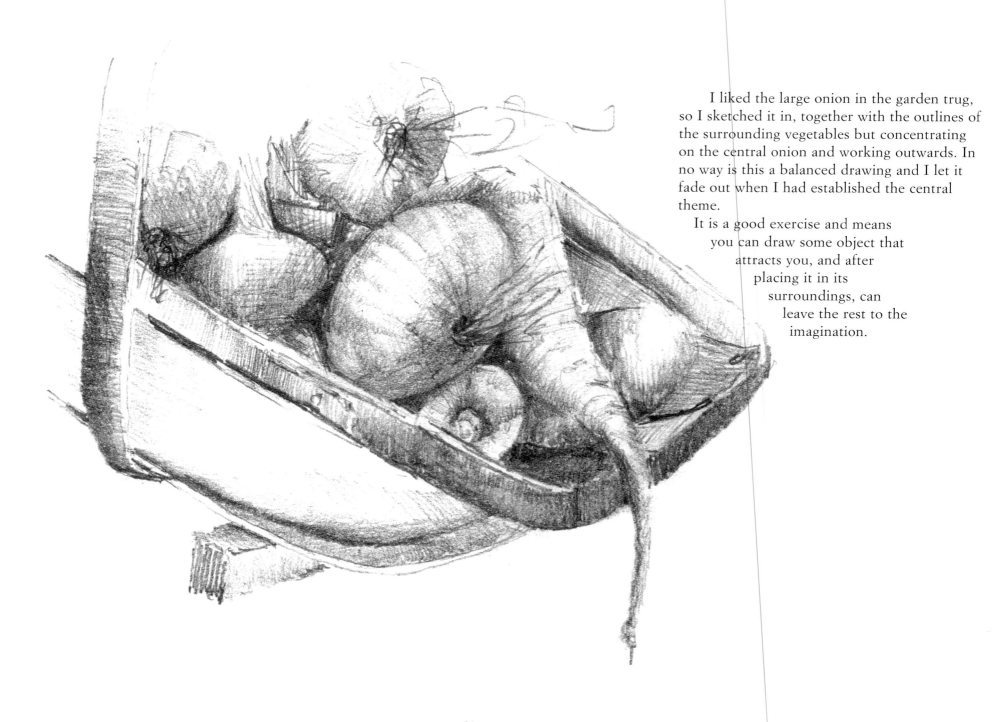

I liked the large onion in the garden trug, so I sketched it in, together with the outlines of the surrounding vegetables but concentrating on the central onion and working outwards. In no way is this a balanced drawing and I let it fade out when I had established the central theme.

It is a good exercise and means you can draw some object that attracts you, and after placing it in its surroundings, can leave the rest to the imagination.

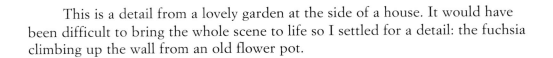

This is a detail from a lovely garden at the side of a house. It would have been difficult to bring the whole scene to life so I settled for a detail: the fuchsia climbing up the wall from an old flower pot.

Neither of these fruits is easy to draw, so why not start off with an outline and only draw a part of them. The pineapple leaves outlined very faintly and the shading was very controlled. You won't compose a masterpiece in the first week, so feel your way slowly.

These little sketches were done during an afternoon and, while they have no particular theme, they are good practice and fun to do.

Before going out into the garden I looked at the back door of a nearby cottage. At first sight, this wooden structure at the back of a cottage might not seem a useful subject for a sketch, but I think it is. The shading inside the door gives a feeling of depth, and you will notice that I have decided to leave out the detail in the foreground to the right of the path, which was green grass.

Try to avoid the temptation to fiddle with extra shading; it is not necessary and will spoil your drawing.

Once again I suggest that before you attempt a complete sketch of your home from the outside, you spend a little time on details of the building. Just fill a page with simple sketches. They will be a pleasing addition to your sketch book and will make you think about structure, but more important still, they will give you confidence.

A corner with a garden hose. This is a case where you could select a central point—like the hose—and extend the drawing outwards to take in the surrounding flowers.

Try it yourself.

Whether you have a large garden, a small patio or just a window box, it will provide a subject for a sketch. This is a drawing of a very cleverly designed glaze of colour in a minute courtyard. If I had put in all the brickwork and every stem and leaf it would have become top heavy and would have missed the impression of brightness and colour that I wanted to give.

These two pages tell an important story. How far do I take my sketch?

I think I can hear you say: 'That's not all that simple', but in fact it is. You can stop at any stage and it will be a pleasant subject to sketch. Either of these two little pictures could go into your sketch book. Remember how important it is to decide what to leave out. It is all too easy to go on and on until you have spoiled your work with too much detail.

Let me try to convince you that you will have just as much fun sketching smaller details as you will from more complicated set-piece landscape drawings. At this stage choose subjects that are within your ability range. It may be an old shed or a gatepost or a wall, or even a detail from a house. With this more finished sketch I have accentuated parts by shading heavily, and have left other parts relatively light. Remember that shading can create depth.

When tackling this subject, I started by defining the walls and window with a very light touch indeed. To ensure that the light flooded in to the work bench, I worked outwards from the source of light. It was done with a 2B pencil, and darkened at the bottom with a 6B.

Try a complete sketch of the outside of your house — but again, don't aim to produce a 'finished' drawing: the essential features are all that you should attempt at this stage.

Now that your interest is aroused, wherever you go you will find that your eyes are picking up possible subjects for a sketch, and gradually you will become more selective. It is a good idea to stop and look back. You may not find a composition ahead of you, but there may be a wonderful subject right behind you.

Sketching Out of Doors

Now let's start – but **please remember** – you are not going to try anything that is too difficult at first.

You are sitting in the countryside or on a beach and looking at the scene in front of you, trying to make up your mind what you will draw. Here is a hint. Take the outer box of a match box and put it to your eye. Better still cut a rectangle out of a piece of card.

What you see is the area that will fill your page. Have you ever thought that it is only when your eyes concentrate on a particular tree or wall or bush that you are aware of the intricate detail. Otherwise there is only a general form of landscape. So what you decide to leave out is almost as important as what you put in.

Forget the detail for a moment, and consider where you are going to place the horizon in your first sketch.

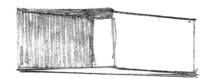

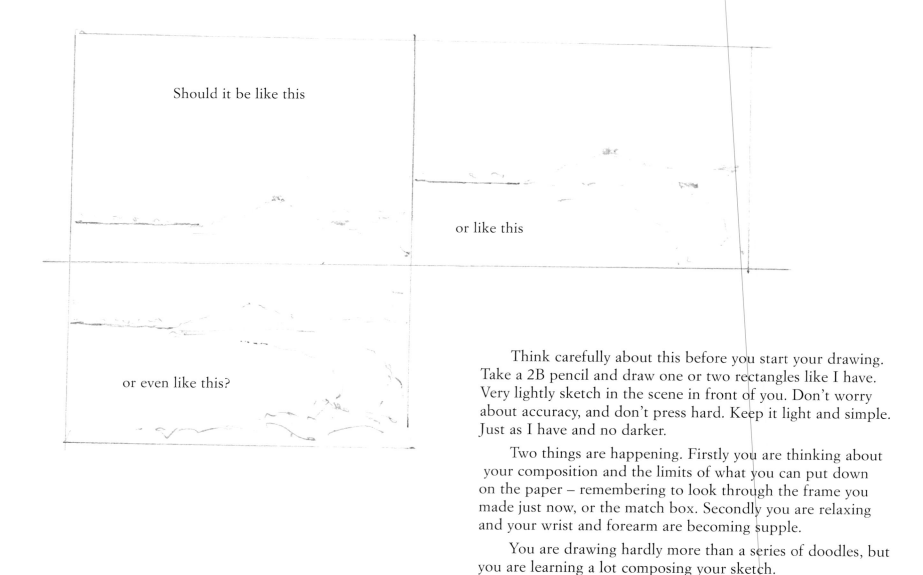

Should it be like this

or like this

or even like this?

Think carefully about this before you start your drawing. Take a 2B pencil and draw one or two rectangles like I have. Very lightly sketch in the scene in front of you. Don't worry about accuracy, and don't press hard. Keep it light and simple. Just as I have and no darker.

Two things are happening. Firstly you are thinking about your composition and the limits of what you can put down on the paper – remembering to look through the frame you made just now, or the match box. Secondly you are relaxing and your wrist and forearm are becoming supple.

You are drawing hardly more than a series of doodles, but you are learning a lot composing your sketch.

You have decided where to place the horizon – in my case a quarter of the way down from the top of the page. It has gone in lightly with a 2B. In this way I can relate the hill, the castle and the foreground to my line of horizon. It is only in outline, and at this stage we are not trying to produce a masterpiece – just a preliminary thumbnail sketch.

The outline is in and we can now start some shading. There are few rules, but in general the further away into the distance you are, the lighter the shading.

I finished the sketch and ended up using a 4B and a 6B pencil in the foreground. Study carefully what I must have left out. There are no clouds and the sea is untouched. I have tried to make a difference between the islands in the distance and the foreground. We are always striving to give a three dimensional effect to a flat surface. This is not a finished drawing – it is a sketch, and I hope you will have great fun and satisfaction in filling your sketch book with the results of your work.

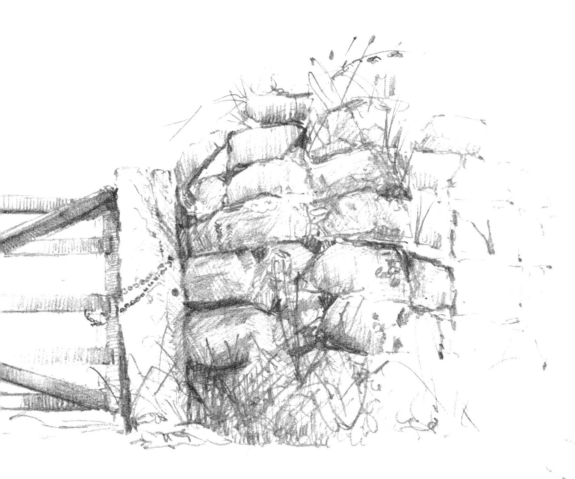

Here is another idea. Instead of looking for a landscape subject, why don't you find something near you. There are masses of subjects right under your nose – a gate post or a tree stump or a dead branch. Perhaps there is a path that leads your eye into the distance, but near at hand an interesting subject to make a pleasing composition. Look for something simple.

Both these sketches were done without moving my stool. I used a 6B pencil only and they were sketched in with the very **lightest** of touch. Notice that the angle at which the shading is applied will help to give substance to the drawing.

It is time to become a little more critical. Study the composition of these two sketches. I didn't have to move very far, but they are both different. In future, I hope that you will be looking at subjects as compositions for a sketch. When you are browsing through your photographs, or indeed when you are about to take a photograph, try to think of compositions. The same is true for reproductions in magazines and books, and when you are looking at a painting. Ask yourself, 'Do I like this composition, or could it be improved?' Now do the same when you are out of doors, and always be on the lookout for a simple but effective composition. When you are considering a subject, move fifty yards to either side and see if the composition is improved. Which part of the scene appeals to you most? In this case, is it the porch or the rose window or the gravestones in the foreground?

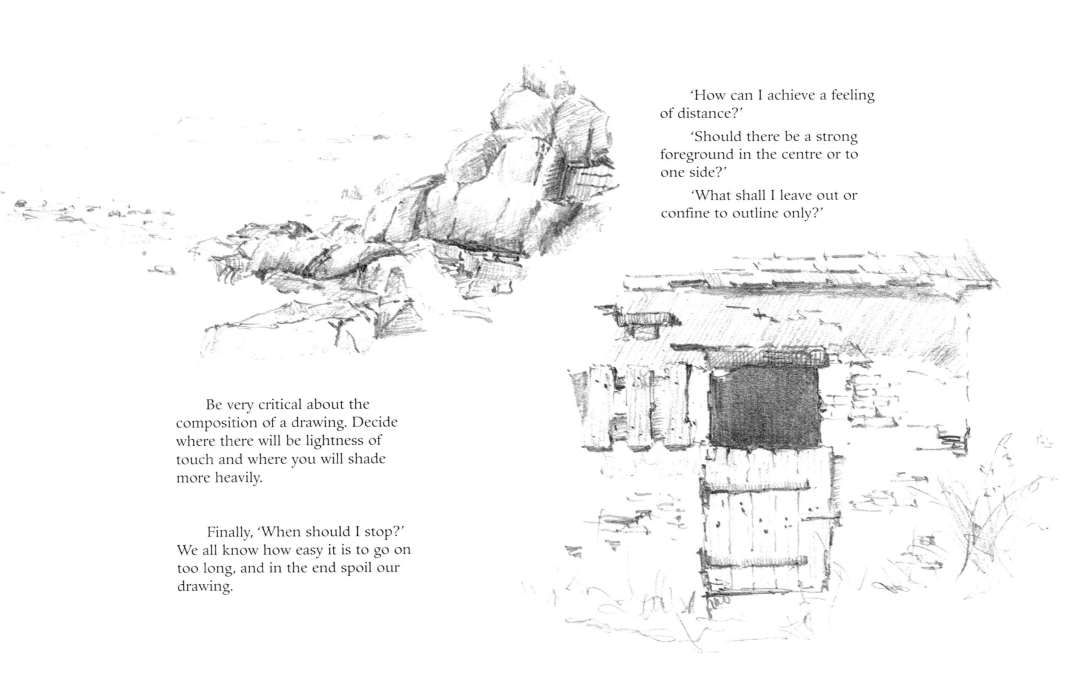

'How can I achieve a feeling of distance?'

'Should there be a strong foreground in the centre or to one side?'

'What shall I leave out or confine to outline only?'

Be very critical about the composition of a drawing. Decide where there will be lightness of touch and where you will shade more heavily.

Finally, 'When should I stop?' We all know how easy it is to go on too long, and in the end spoil our drawing.

If I had drawn the house in detail it would have overshadowed the seat and the old outhouse. Instead, I started by sketching in the main features **very** lightly with a 2B pencil, and then shaded round the seat to bring it forward.

The full strength of my 6B pencil was used round the edge of parts of the seat. Then I tried to give a feeling of separate identity firstly of the seat, then the wall behind it, then the outhouse with its door, and finally the outline of the house.

At this stage I want to reintroduce our old friend PERSPECTIVE. It can be a little daunting, but I want to suggest some very basic thoughts. Firstly, objects tend to converge and diminish as they recede into the distance. When they actually disappear at the horizon, they are said to have reached the vanishing point. A line of trees or a railway track are good examples of this.

As we have seen, your eye level dictates the position of the horizon. It can be anywhere on a sketch but it will affect your drawing in every way. These three examples show what happens when you are below your subject, and looking up at it; when you are level with it; and when you are above it. Don't be put off by these problems, for it's early days yet. The most important task is to keep confident and enthusiastic about your drawing. I will introduce perspective from time to time – and provided you spend a little time trying to understand that it is a natural part of your drawing, I don't think it will prove too difficult.

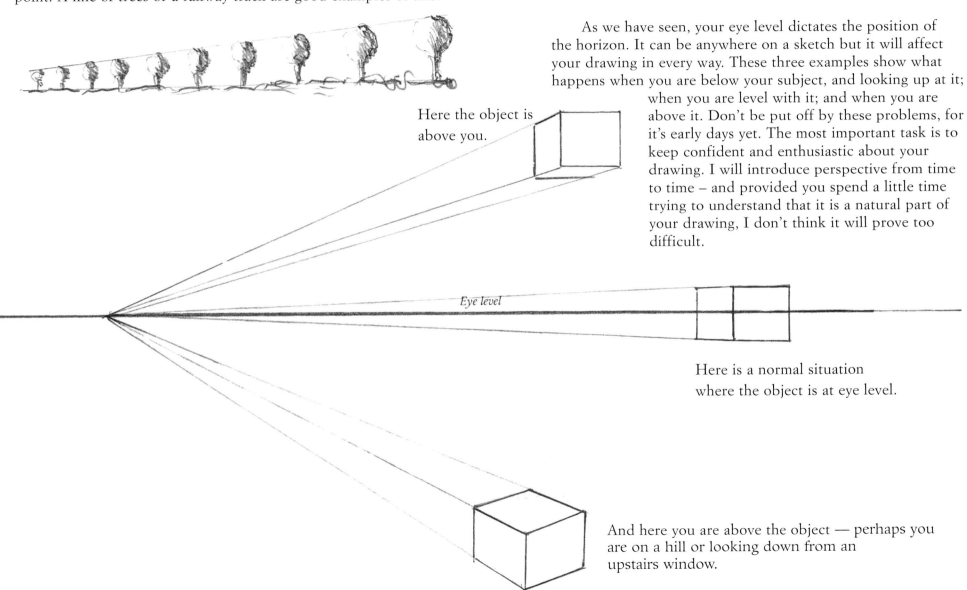

Here the object is above you.

Eye level

Here is a normal situation where the object is at eye level.

And here you are above the object — perhaps you are on a hill or looking down from an upstairs window.

We will start now with a collection of buildings. You may be in the country or in a town, but the principle is the same. Think from where you would like to sit to do your drawing. You are composing your pictures, and I hope using your matchbox or viewer. try to keep it simple and maybe do one or two light drawings to block in where the outline and rooftops will come. A light line across the page to show the eye level and thus the vanishing points will save you a lot of problems. Here are some step by step stages from a drawing.

Spend a moment or two looking at this drawing. If I had included the granite stone in the end wall of the facing cottage it would have destroyed the feeling of sunlight (which is accentuated by the shadows). The cottage in the distance on the left is brought to life with the shrubs and trees that surround it. The roadway is in sunlight and the boats are a lucky composition bonus. Note that I have only given the barest indication of the granite wall on the right. Finally – there was no need to make any shading in the sky. This is what I mean by deciding what to leave out.

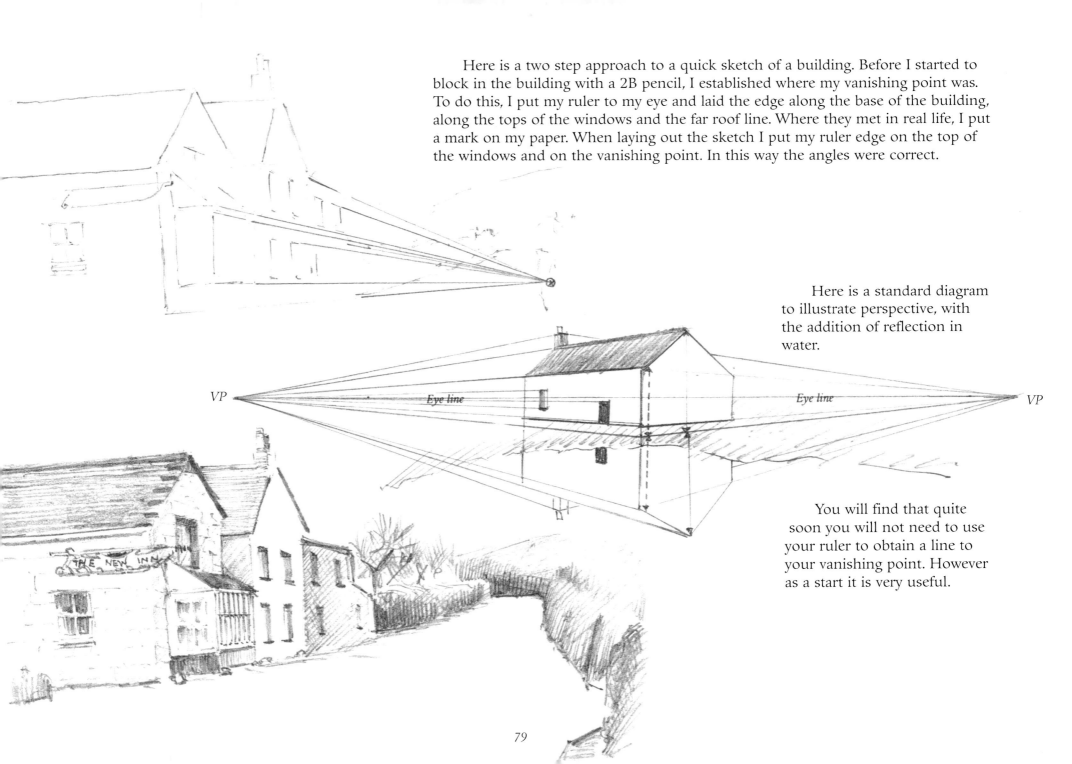

Here is a two step approach to a quick sketch of a building. Before I started to block in the building with a 2B pencil, I established where my vanishing point was. To do this, I put my ruler to my eye and laid the edge along the base of the building, along the tops of the windows and the far roof line. Where they met in real life, I put a mark on my paper. When laying out the sketch I put my ruler edge on the top of the windows and on the vanishing point. In this way the angles were correct.

Here is a standard diagram to illustrate perspective, with the addition of reflection in water.

VP

Eye line

Eye line

VP

You will find that quite soon you will not need to use your ruler to obtain a line to your vanishing point. However as a start it is very useful.

THE NEW INN

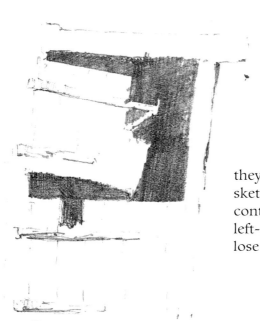

Contrasts in shading —
they could both go into your
sketch book, but if you
continued to shade the
left-hand sketch you might
lose some of the lightness.

The collection of barns sketched on the opposite page gives further examples of what to accentuate and what to leave out. The roof of the farmhouse on the left remains in outline only, while the trees behind the cowshed roof are very dark. They push the roofs forward. There is no need to try to draw every branch of the trees. Not only will it be very difficult but it will probably result in them becoming overpowering. Remember that in real life you don't see all the details – it is only when your eye rests on an object that you actually **see** the individual twigs and small branches. In this case you are looking at a scene.

81

Shading is all important. I think that you will be helped if, as you draw, you fix your thoughts on how you can obtain a feeling of depth three dimensionally. Think to yourself 'I need to bring this part forward, so I must leave the background unshaded for the moment, and accentuate one part so that it stands out'.

Don't worry, it will all come with practice.

This half completed sketch of the other side of the gateway brings out one or two more points. A very light touch with an HB pencil has blocked in the outlines. I used my rubber two or three times before I got the proportions correct. The decision about what to leave out must now be taken. The big fir tree on the left is helping to bring the building forward – but the effect will be lost if we shade the building too much.

How can I get a feeling of distance when looking through the gateway? Possibly either by deep shading inside the gateway and suggesting trees visible on the left through the archway. However I would lose everything if there was too much detail and it became fussy.

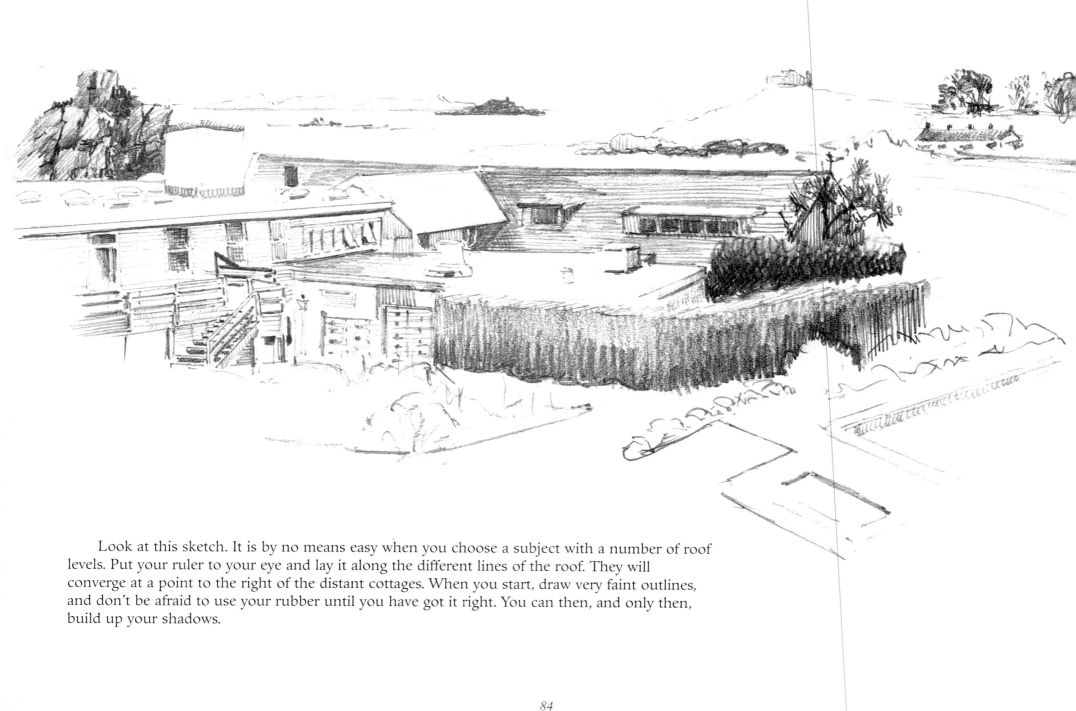

Look at this sketch. It is by no means easy when you choose a subject with a number of roof levels. Put your ruler to your eye and lay it along the different lines of the roof. They will converge at a point to the right of the distant cottages. When you start, draw very faint outlines, and don't be afraid to use your rubber until you have got it right. You can then, and only then, build up your shadows.

Here are two illustrations of distance.
In this drawing the road disappears round a bend.

And in this one strong foreground shading gives
way to a lighter touch in the distance.

Trees

Trees are wonderful subjects for sketching and, having grasped one or two basic ideas, are not too difficult. Light and shade are the whole basis of drawing trees. Unless your eye dwells on a particular tree or clump you will not register much detail, whereas a further glance will take in the branches and finally every twig. This can all be achieved in your drawing. Some people will want to draw with a fine outline and the result will be totally satisfying, while others will seek to use al the pencils in the range. Some will want to put in every details and some will achieve their results with shading alone. Sunlight and shadow are all important in producing the effect you want. Here are some examples.

And here are some more.

You don't have to move far among trees to find a wealth of subjects, and the pages of your sketch book can be filled with small but very expressive and satisfying individual drawings.

Here are two more suggestions.

The trees in the distance are no more than a block of shading with no detail, with the darker trees in front there is a feeling of distance. Half close your eyes and see that distant detail is unnecessary.

Here we have various methods of shading. Try using different pencils and shade at different angles. Think about light and shade.

The mighty oak opposite comes from a park. I sketched in the skeleton of the tree first and tried to visualise it in mid winter without its leaves. For the shading I used two pencils 2B and 4B. If when sketching you half close your eyes for a moment, you will only see massed as opposed to individual leaves and this will help to avoid too much detail.

Finally I used my rubber where I wanted highlights, but with very short strokes. I cleaned it after every stroke.

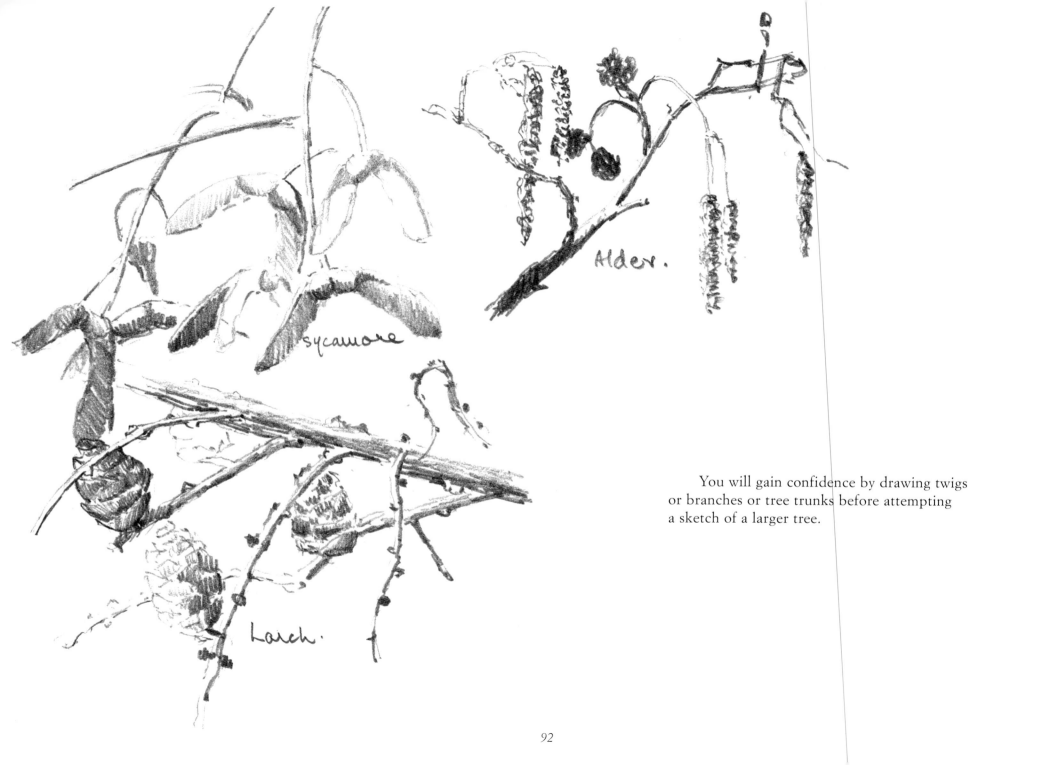

Alder.

sycamore

Larch.

You will gain confidence by drawing twigs
or branches or tree trunks before attempting
a sketch of a larger tree.

Here are some further examples of trees and branches.

Twigs can be great fun and hugely rewarding.

A few brief words about clouds and the sky. Clouds are fascinating but they can so easily dominate the drawing even if they are not meant to. They can always be built up, so treat them very lightly until you have sensed the correct balance for the picture. Look at the two sketches above. The sketch on the left is rather overbalanced by the strength of the sky.

The one on the right is better I think. However in the sketch on the opposite page the clouds are the dominant feature and the branches of the tree are being blown by the wind. A 6B pencil was used and the whole of the sky shaded in diagonal lines. A touch here and there with my rubber formed the softness of the clouds, then heavier shading strengthened the drawing.

We should spend a little more time on composition. It will make all the difference to your drawing.

Spend a little time walking about to find the best spot where the balance between foreground and distance is right.

Very often there is a key object in the foreground or middle distance and if you put it in the centre of the drawing you may have problems.

Remember that the viewer's eye wants to be taken into the picture and not out of it. For instance, if you include a flock of gulls, I suggest that they are flying into the picture and not flying out of the right hand side.

The Seashore

Sketching from the beach presents endless possibilities and can give you many hours of enjoyment. Whether it is a view of the harbour or the sand dunes or rocks on the foreshore or even distant islands, the principle is the same.

Decide on your line of horizon.

Set out your vanishing points – if there are buildings.

Remember that you are going to convey a feeling of distance.

Plan your sketch with some small rectangles – decide on the best composition and how much you can fit in (put the cut-out rectangle or matchbox top to your eye).

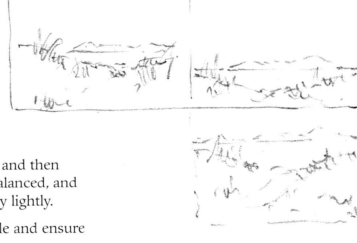

Make a start by sketching in very lightly the main features, and then strengthen them with some shading. Try to keep the drawing balanced, and get a feeling of distance by outlining features in the horizon very lightly.

I am sure you are going to enjoy yourself, but keep it simple and ensure that your pencils are sharp.

Here is a simple sketch done at low water.

Try to have some of your pages filled with details. It is not only good practice, but it is a delightful reminder of a happy afternoon's sketching. Notice the shading in these sketches. I used a 2B pencil very lightly to draw in the outline and then a 4B.

You will find that in general you are sketching a calm sea. Think before you put in too much shading. It may help to accentuate the sea, but again in many cases it will cause you problems. As a start I suggest you leave the viewer to recognise the sea, and avoid heavy shading.

Try to avoid tackling too much in your drawing. These two pages are simple, but it will help you to gain confidence if you realise that lightness can be conveyed by leaving out much of the finer detail.

I wanted to sketch from where I was sitting, but it wasn't a good composition. There is no obvious focal point which draws your eye (despite an attempt to use birds). I moved a few yards down the beach and the next sketch is more balanced.

The heavily shaded boat in this quick sketch helps to give a feeling of distance.

The direction of the pencil work in this drawing helps to give a feeling of movement.

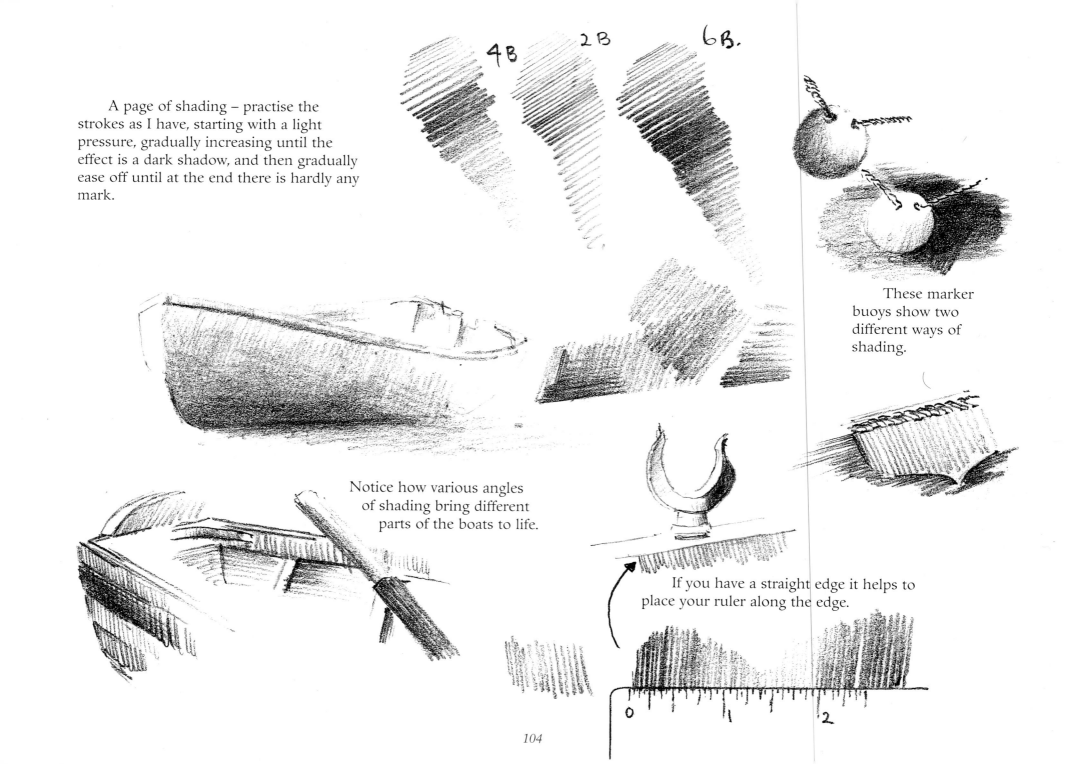

A page of shading – practise the strokes as I have, starting with a light pressure, gradually increasing until the effect is a dark shadow, and then gradually ease off until at the end there is hardly any mark.

4B 2B 6B.

These marker buoys show two different ways of shading.

Notice how various angles of shading bring different parts of the boats to life.

If you have a straight edge it helps to place your ruler along the edge.

0   1   2

104

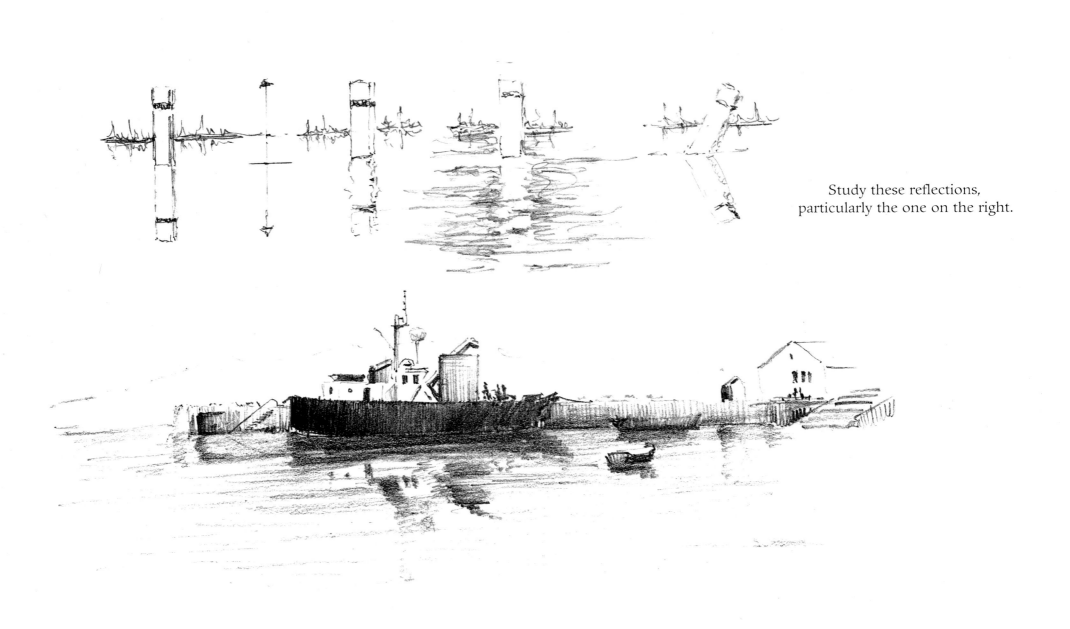

Study these reflections,
particularly the one on the right.

On the opposite page I have made a quick series of sketches to explain reflection. The top left hand sketch of posts in still water shows, in the left hand post, that the reflection is the same height as the post. The next post is in ruffled water but the outline is still there. The stick, on the other hand, is at an angle and the reflection is directly below the stick. Turn the page upside down and look at the mirror image.

The barges tied up on the opposite bank are in completely still water and the reflection is an exact replica, while the beached barge is on sand with puddles which give an intermittent reflection in the water. The reflection breaks off where the sand is present.

On the opposite page is St Michael's Mount. I suggested to you that it is probably better to place any dominating feature in the foreground or middle distance away from the centre. In this drawing I've done the opposite which only goes to show that there are exceptions at times. Of course in this case the Mount is in the distance and is the subject of the painting. Try placing a book to the left or right of the sketch to block off a part to see if the composition could be improved. It seems to me to be about right.

Rocks present problems and sometimes it isn't easy to produce that feeling of sheer bulk and roundness. One way is to vary your shading from leaving the paper blank to using a 4 or 6B pencil.

I want to keep plugging away at you about lightness of touch. Everyone has their own method of working, but whereas with watercolours and oil paints the colour can tell the story, here the pencil has to do it all.

These boats tied up to the quay were not easy and the very faint outline drawing had to be corrected quite a lot before I began shading. The problem is when to stop. I began by building up the reflections but have left it as it is. The water and sky are now a part of your imagination. You may wish to have a completely different treatment which is perfectly valid, but it is wide to start with a light touch.

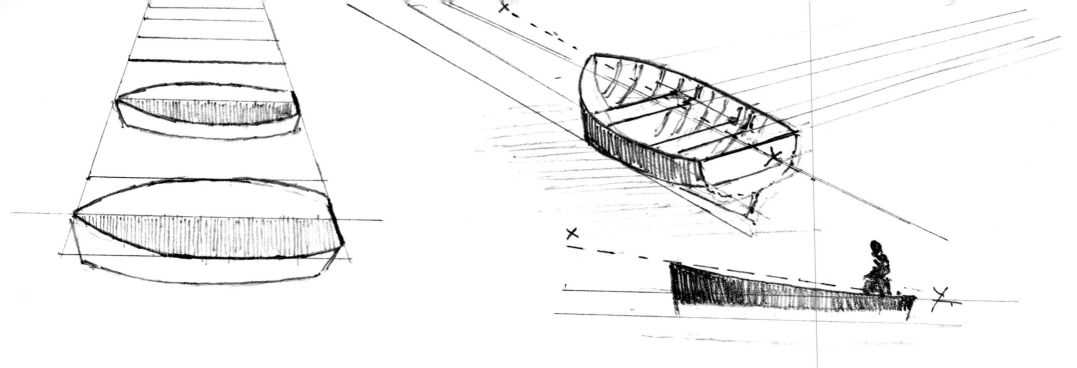

Small boats are attractive subjects, so it is important to understand the principles of perspective. It is not difficult, as we know lines move to one or more vanishing points at eye level.

In the left hand drawing one boat is further away than the other, as you can see. What may not be quite so obvious is that the nearer shaded half of each boat is slightly larger than the other half. This is because the unshaded half is further away.

In the right hand drawing there are two vanishing points. Because the boat is lower in the water and the flare of the bow is pronounced, the bow is higher than the stern, as shown on the lines XY.

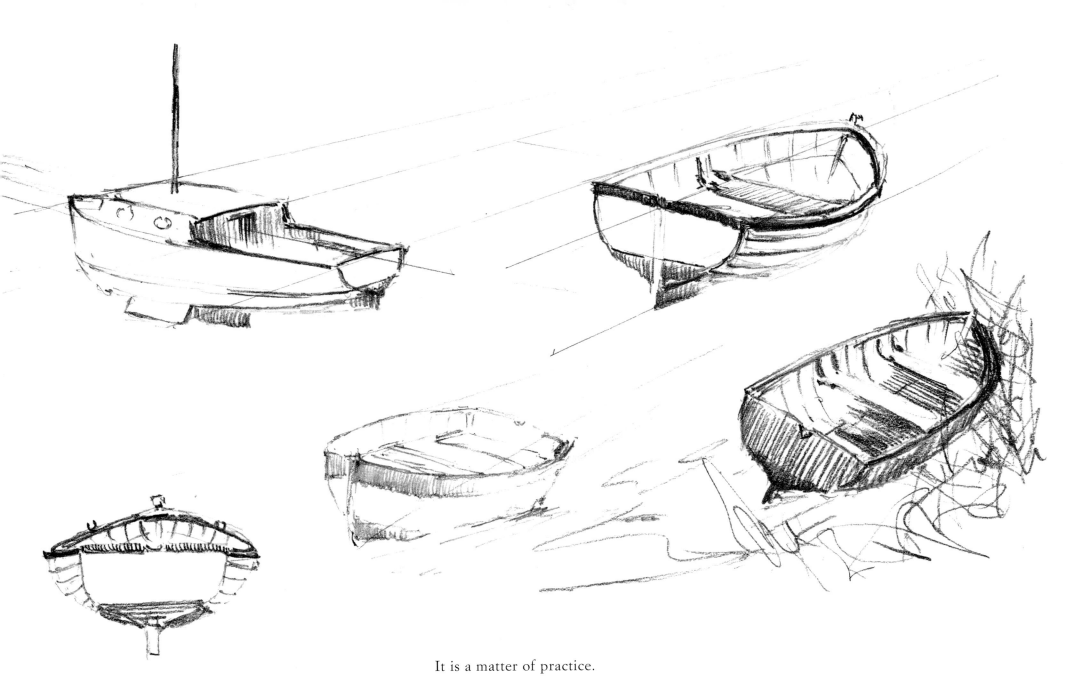

It is a matter of practice.

In the beginning there is a great opportunity 'above the tide line' either on holiday or if you live near the sea.

The golden rule must be to select subjects within your present field of understanding. These two items were on the quay at Newlyn. Look at them carefully.

I used my rubber to overcome problems of accuracy and didn't bother with the rest of the quay or the trawlers alongside. It was just a study in shading and started with a barely visible outline with an HB pencil. When I had got it right I used a 2B to build up the shading. Notice from where the light was coming.

Here are some ideas which you can tackle. The simplest subjects when filling a page of your sketch book will give a lot of pleasure.

When I was drawing this faint outline I used my rubber to correct mistakes, and my shading picked up darker areas all over the drawing. It is not a question of finishing the top left corner and working down – it is better to build up the shading in all parts of the sketch before we imagine depth and the third dimension. Be careful not to overdo the shading or you may be left with no highlights. Finally, I used my rubber to put a reflective shine on some of the lobster pot floats.

I was first attracted to the window by the colour – the floats were white, yellow, red and orange and made a wonderful subject for a painting against the granite wall.

This may seem to have been difficult. It isn't really.
I sat on a wall and **very** lightly drew in the window and the
surrounding stonework, just the outline.

Inland rivers are normally calm and provide the most marvellous subject for sketching. Here the river Avon in Hampshire is a perfect example. This little drawing, which did not take long, has one or two points worth noting:–

The sky is left blank.

The river is left blank.

The distant hills are in outline only.

The trees are strongly reflected in the water.

I used the edge of my rubber to touch the paper in order to show the edge of the water at the bottom of the river bank.

The foreground is quite strong and dark and forms a natural edge to the bottom of the sketch.

The bottom right hand side is left completely blank.

In this way your imagination fills in the gaps and the composition provides a feeling of distance and serenity.

Here is quite a different treatment. There is a feeling of still water but it is deeply shaded with reflections from surrounding trees.

From the pencil strokes you will see that I worked fast with 2B and 4B pencils and there is an abrupt change from dark to completely white paper.

In reality there were primroses covering the grass on the edge of the river,and the reeds had died back during the winter. Go for simplicity and again, it is worth half closing your eyes to blur every little detail.

Sketching in Towns and Cities

Perhaps you live in a town and don't have the chance easily to sketch in the countryside. There is a wealth of interest and you can have great fun – provided you approach your work as we have done throughout the book. Start by looking at buildings or compositions as subjects for sketching. You may not want to sit on a stool in the High Street, so find a seat and look all round. Perhaps you are sitting in your car, which is an admirable place to remain incognito while you sketch. Don't feel that you must sketch the whole of a scene – it's not necessary.

Look out of the window at home and see if there is a chimney pot in view. They are simple, don't take long and give you practice in shading and proportions – so don't despise the chimney pot.

At some stage you will want to draw the outside of your house — an interesting exercise and not without its perspective problems. Suppose you start off by sitting at a window and select some simple sketch to start with. I chose the chimney pots on surrounding houses.

Rooftops and chimney pots never fail to capture my interest.
There's a whole landscape up there above the houses, bursting with
fascinating shapes, angles, textures, light and shade, all of it
wonderful material for your sketch book. And just think how few
people ever bother to look! Good drawing is as much about
observation, learning to look and see, as it is about practice.
The two go together well.

Practise drawing your house from different angles,
leaving the adjoining buildings to fade out.

Windows and doorways often have interesting architectural details and make lively studies for your sketch book. Keep an eye open for the unusual, and make a habit of sketching it when you find it. Remember to use your sketch books as a resource for your more ambitious drawings – borrow details and ideas whenever a new composition demands it. Among the details on these two pages, note how panes of glass, above right, come to life when they reflect the light outside.

Part 2
Sketching Indoors

Starting at home

The idea of just sitting down and starting to sketch out of the blue, even in your own living room, is a little daunting. It helps if you begin with the ordinary, so set aside a short set time, say half an hour, to take yourself on a brief visual journey through your home and to sketch something that attracts you. Don't worry at this stage about composition or design; try to focus on a corner with a few objects that have simple shapes. Feel free in a sketchbook to simplify and edit a scene, or (when occasion demands) investigate something very thoroughly.

To isolate an image imagine you are looking through a camera lens; just as you would when taking a photo, aim to avoid the distraction of the rest of the room. One way of making this easier is to make a cut-out viewfinder from a piece of card.

When you start a sketch you should have an aim in mind, but this often changes: you may find yourself embarking on a sketch only as a means of jotting down information to find that it ends up being a stimulus for a large painting.

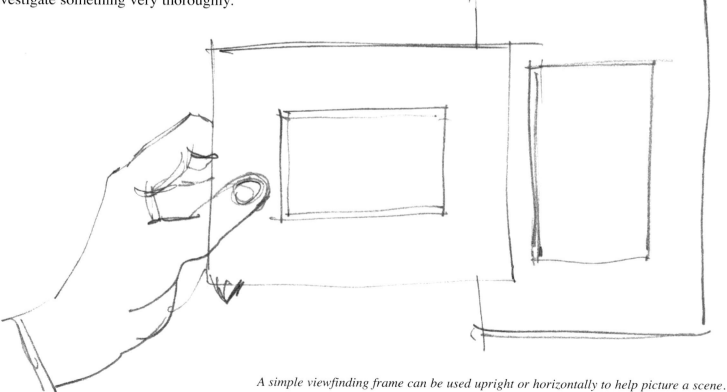

A simple viewfinding frame can be used upright or horizontally to help picture a scene.

The living room

Here, I have chosen to sketch a corner of a table, a chair, and the suggestion of a plant, using a 2B pencil.

Mark out very lightly the important points of the general structure. The plant pot's height, the shape and height of the chair and the surface of the table all need to be gently established from the start. To get some sense of scale, use a pencil held vertically at arm's length to 'measure' the proportions of one item in relation to another. Indoors you are never dealing with huge distances, but the size and angle of the table edge and the slight enlarging of the nearer handle create a sense of depth.

I used a touch of hatching to give the cushion solidity and to indicate the cure on the leg of the table. The sketch has no edges - what you leave out is just as important as what you put in.

127

The kitchen

The kitchen is often the heart of the house, and signs of life make for lively sketching. I found plenty of things to sketch in my own and friends' kitchens.

In the sketch of the Aga all the tea towels drying and the array of kitchen utensils hanging overhead added interest, and the brickwork gave the sketch a strong structure.
This was sketched with an HB pencil, the underlying fine lines put in first with very light pressure to give a skeleton to work upon. Personally, I don't mind these showing through the final sketch - the skill of a clean contour line can be honed later. Again, proportions can be assessed with the help of a pencil held up to the scene. As the lines are mainly horizontal and vertical, like a grid, the rest fitted over quite easily. I shaded the areas in shadow, such as the side of the cooker, with crosshatching.

In another kitchen I was interested in the view out towards the hall, and wanted to include the drying herbs hanging over the doorway. I used a waterproof rollerball and ink diluted to make a wash for the shadows, pushing the ink wash around with a brush. Don't plunge into the darkest shadows first, wait until you are more confident in judging the different relationships of tone: work from the lightest wash and build up into the darkest areas, in this case under the door. In this sketch there is an element of perspective to take into account; this will be tackled later (see pages 140-141).

Work rooms

I drew my studio and a friend's music room, but you might just as easily focus on the washing machine, your desk, a wall of tools or the interior of a garden shed.

I chose a very soft charcoal pencil to suggest the piano against the window, and only barely hinted at what can be seen outside the window.

My studio was a lightning sketch with brush and watercolour. It was looking relatively tidy and so speed was both my choice and a knowledge that it would not look so neat for long! (Having said that, the messy evidence of people also makes interesting sketching).

The bedroom

A bedroom scene gives a very intimate view
of the owner, so look for little signs that are
intriguing and attractive. Here, the dressing
gown is the focal point, the bed itself left as
a simple shape, although I paid attention to
the pillows and how they sat. It took only a few
lines to indicate the gathers. The paleness of the
bed linen is emphasized by its contrast to
the bedhead.

Using a brush and grey watercolour gives a
wobbly, fluid line, which is the major difference
in exchanging your pencil for wet materials.
The light was going, so I had to put a spurt on
and I think this sketch benefits from a casual
treatment - perhaps the essence of successful
sketching is to look hard and give the study
some thought, so that less is more when it comes
to the actual physical drawing.

This very quick sketch of the chest of drawers
was made with an art pen, brush and water.
Soften lines by just running the brush against
the line. The effect can also be useful for covering mistakes: when you abandon the pencil you
also lose the ability to erase. But it's only a
sketch, so plunge in and experiment.

132

The bathroom

My bathroom is unremarkable so I had low expectations of it, but a few little sketches of the shower curtain and some towels kept me happy. They turned into little studies of how fabric hangs and where shadows fall in the folds. The shadows will be more obvious where the folds are sharpest. Start by putting in the essential points and gradually build up.

Grainy watercolour paper gripped the rather powdery charcoal pencil I used here, and successfully conveyed the texture of the towel. At the end I erased to bring out the highlights.

For the towel hanging on the back of the door I used a 4B pencil and used the side of the pencil to make the shadows. It is worth noting what happens to pattern when folded or rumpled – here the stripes drop diagonally into folds – as an indication of pattern like this makes all the difference to a convincing rendition.

The shower curtain was a swift, bold pencil sketch, concentrating on the effect of the stiff folds. The 'negative shape' of the shadow behind (the curtain is the 'positive shape') gives the curtain substance and makes the folds stand out. (There is more on negative and positive shapes on pages 148-149).

A friend's bathroom proved much more exciting, especially as the cat decided to play a starring part. I had to be very quick - in a circumstance like this, get the cat down on paper even if you are concentrating on the taps at the time. The cat's arrival really altered the focus of the sketch and exploited the view from the window. I kept to line (I was working with a pencil) as there were so may horizontals and verticals that introducing tone would have made a confused image.

The conservatory

If like me, you don't have a conservatory, you may have friends who do (and who will probably be thrilled and flattered by your interest), and there are always public gardens to explore. This might mean 'going public', so choose a moment when you are feeling confident and undaunted.

The composition of this pencil drawing was carefully designed to exploit the length of the conservatory. The hinted-at chair in the foreground leads the eye into the picture, to cross the depth suggested by the diminishing sizes of the floor tiles and through to the doorway outside. Composition of a sketch and tackling perspective are looked at next.

Composition

A sketchbook is really a vehicle for trying out ideas, and is the ideal place to work out the layout and composition of future paintings and drawings.

The first decision is whether to draw in a landscape (horizontal) or portrait (vertical) format on the paper. A viewfinder will help you to choose which is more effective for a particular scene, but pay attention, as well, to your intuition.

Choosing to sketch a whole room or a small intimate corner will create images with completely different moods, as will the viewpoint you choose. Move around a room, noting how sitting or standing affects your viewpoint. A high viewpoint can open up a sketch and give a sense of space. A normal viewpoint, i.e. at eye level standing up, gives a familiar perspective. A low viewpoint will affect the objects nearer to you, making them bolder. Try this out by looking at the same view from a standing, sitting and finally a lying-down position.

Here are three obviously different eye levels to sketch from. Try and be comfortable, but do try all of them out before you start and choose the best view.

Two alternative views of the same image.

137

This very simple pure line pencil sketch was made while standing up in a corner of the room and takes in almost the whole kitchen.

This brush and watercolour sketch was made while sitting on the stairs, looking down and focusing only on the left-hand side of the room.

This sketch (again in pencil) was also made from the stairs, but slightly lower down and taking in the other side of the room. Notice what happens to the circular table and the floor tile pattern.

The example above introduces us neatly to the topic of perspective.

Perspective

Perspective is a method conveying the appearance of distance and three dimensions on to a flat, two-dimensional surface such as paper.

In the previous two sketches of the kitchen, my viewpoint had changed and, with it, my horizon. All receding lines below my eye level (the floor tiles, the edge of the dresser) rise to meet my horizon and, if you were to extend

them on and on, would meet at what is called the 'vanishing point', often out of the picture. In the sketch on page 129, the same effect occurs with the tops of the cupboards above my eye level: if extended they would converge downwards to the same vanishing point as the floorboards and cupboard bottoms.

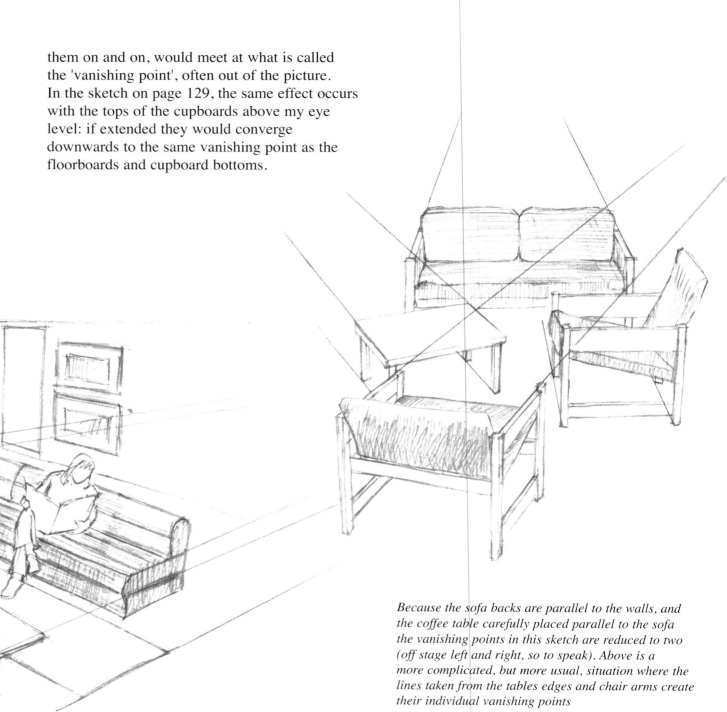

Because the sofa backs are parallel to the walls, and the coffee table carefully placed parallel to the sofa the vanishing points in this sketch are reduced to two (off stage left and right, so to speak). Above is a more complicated, but more usual, situation where the lines taken from the tables edges and chair arms create their individual vanishing points

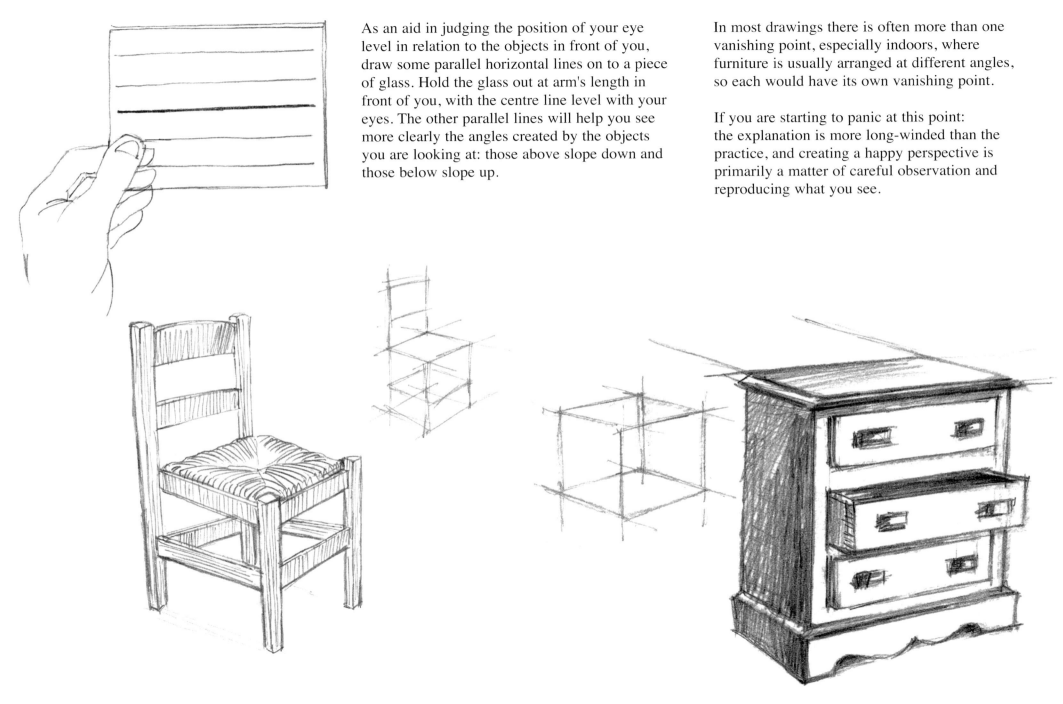

As an aid in judging the position of your eye level in relation to the objects in front of you, draw some parallel horizontal lines on to a piece of glass. Hold the glass out at arm's length in front of you, with the centre line level with your eyes. The other parallel lines will help you see more clearly the angles created by the objects you are looking at: those above slope down and those below slope up.

In most drawings there is often more than one vanishing point, especially indoors, where furniture is usually arranged at different angles, so each would have its own vanishing point.

If you are starting to panic at this point: the explanation is more long-winded than the practice, and creating a happy perspective is primarily a matter of careful observation and reproducing what you see.

Shape and form

Everything we see around can be simplified into a series of basic shapes. Start looking at the shapes of objects without taking into account the effect of how light hits forms and creates shadows. This will help you to understand the structure of quite complicated household items. The most obvious shapes are cubes and spheres. When you start to draw, try to see objects in these terms. You are really looking at the curves and straight lines of contours. When drawing these, try not to use a ruler.

The information on perspective (pages 140-141) is a basic insight into how simple cube shapes, such as chests of drawers, chairs, tables and beds are a series of parallel sides that, when transferred to two-dimensional shapes on paper, have line that converge at a vanishing point.

Slightly more complex to draw are rounded objects such as circular tables, bowls, bottles, plant pots etc. The core shape is an ellipse, a foreshortened circle that will change its proportions according to your eye level.

To draw an ellipse, take a horizontal line as the middle of your shape. Cut it down the middle with a vertical. Draw a curved line over the horizontal so it is equally bisected by the vertical, then draw its mirror image below the horizontal. The depth of the ellipse will present a varying viewpoint of a rounded object.

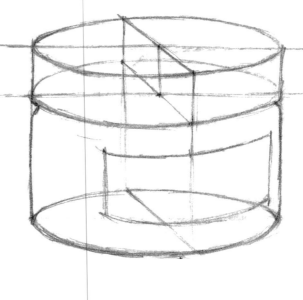

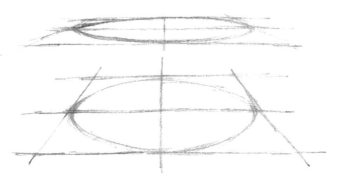

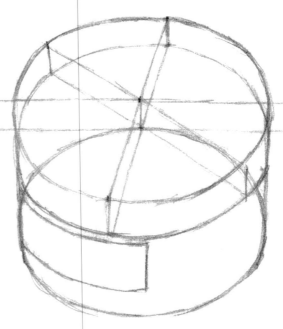

Develop this idea for drawing a bottle. Draw a vertical as the middle of the bottle, then a horizontal across the shoulders of the bottle before they narrow into the neck. Then draw both sides of the bottle simultaneously and note the depth of the ellipse at the mouth of the bottle and at the base. Do the same exercise with a tumbler, a steamed glass, a bowl ... anything that breaks down into basic ellipses. Master it and you will have learnt how to construct a challenging shape and one that will occur again and again in sketches which focus on the details of rooms and all the objects that clutter up our homes.

EYE LEVEL

Light and shade

Without dismissing pure line drawing, when an object is drawn in line only the information conveyed about its form is limited. In practice it is almost impossible to separate shape and form from light and shade - everything is affected by light and shade, and the key to depicting this is in degrees of darkness and light, known as tonal values. By simulating the effect of light falling on a surface and using tone to show where shadows fall, you can create the illusion of three-dimensional form.

Light can change quickly, noticeably affecting the appearance of things, so when sketching you will have to take this into account, Either work quickly or make notes on the angle and strength of light or, more daringly, make several sketches showing the effect of the changing light.

When concentrating on tone, your sketches will tend to become moodier and more atmospheric; try to avoid too many detailed lines and emphasize shapes and forms. Limiting yourself to three degrees of tone to start with will help you look closely for strong shapes and tonal contrasts. Squinting through half-closed eyes will help reduce a complicated interior to a simplified range of tones.

For the sketch on the left I used charcoal for a darker-shadowed, less defined look, adding a few final highlights by erasing. The sketch below is a watercolour, noticeably more fluid and with more marked and yet more subtle degrees of light and shade.

Experimenting with tone is also a chance to expand into different materials and have fun with the variety of possible effects. The sketch on the previous page was done with a 2B pencil, the first degree of shading done by hatching, and darker areas emphasized with cross-hatching.

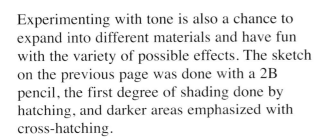

The large windows in this grand London house let in wonderful shafts of light from both sides, creating interesting areas of light and shadow on the floor. The columns are a good example of how shading works to depict a curved surface. The shade is indicated by hatching and as the paper was very smooth the pencil slid with ease over the surface.

The conservatory was a perfect place to show the effect of light on an interior. I used pencil for the architectural structure and for some of the areas of tone. A further ink wash worked best for the looser shadows. Be bold in leaving the paper white for the lightest zones.

Details and interesting corners

As you observe and sketch, you will probably be diverted by delightful groupings of all the personal paraphernalia of a house's inhabitants. Kitchen utensils, china, plants, packets of detergent, they are all made up of those basic shapes discussed on pages 142-143, so you are well equipped to tackle interesting corners.

If you need to practise ellipses, then something like the delicate perfume bottles on the bathroom shelf would be an ideal subject. I was inspired by the faceted transparent glass and the unusual shapes. I chose a 2B pencil because the pattern of the objects and the way they overlapped was suitable for treatment in line only. The basket's woven texture was just suggested by sharp repeated lines to indicate the overall pattern - there was no need to fill it all in. Notice how the bottles on the top shelf have narrow ellipses and those on the lower shelf are rounder because they are further below my eye level. I like the way the tap and sink slide out of the picture.

Another shelf with a set of baskets and patterned jugs was an opportunity for sketching in pen, ink and wash. Both sketches demanded I look closely at the shapes between the objects. These 'negative shapes' are as important as the more obvious shapes of the objects themselves – turning the sketch upside down will help you see them not just as background white paper. The relationship of one shape against another becomes important, so you are not putting each down unrelated, like a shopping list. The perfume bottles (above) are another good example of how attention to the proportion of these negative shapes makes it an airy and open design, echoing the transparency of the bottles. The pen and wash (far right) has less area of negative shape and the feel is much more dense. If you focus on both sets of shapes when sketching, the chances are you will produce a better balanced drawing.

This very modest plant study is a mono-chromatic watercolour sketch in a limited range of tones. The negative shape of the dark leaves behind the fern reveal the light side of the pot. I had to be careful to remember to leave the paper bare for the lightest areas.

I couldn't resist the inclusion of a pile of shoes I saw flung on the floor - they are such interesting shapes. I am sure your children, friends' children or grandchildren have trainers, sports shoes, rollerblades or skates all flung on the floor. Not to mention clothes! These sketches were done with a brush line and a touch of tone.

Homes are so full of marvellous little vignettes they could fill several sketchbooks – this section could expand into a whole book. Here are just a few more:

• Bathrooms are always full of interesting details. The toothbrushes and old fashioned taps are part of a simple sketch that was done in a matter of minutes with a fine fibre-tipped pen.

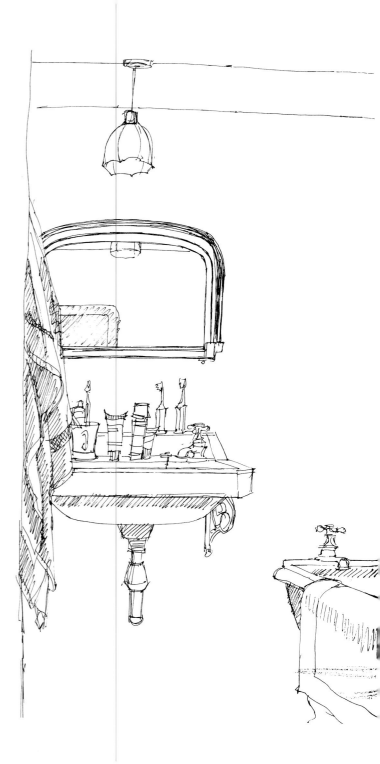

- Containers of dried food are always good subjects, and the patterns of the contents always so different. These were sketched with a fibre-tipped pen.

- The enormous variety of plates, teapots, cups and saucers on dressers are also full of rich pattern. In this pen and water-soluble ink sketch I left the swirls and squiggles rip, to translate rather than copy.

Other settings

Now you are seated by the sketching opportunities in your own home, or even someone else's, it is time to move on to 'public' interiors.

Surrounded by the general public you will probably be desperately trying to make yourself invisible, so start where you are likely to feel most comfortable. Personally, I would choose a café, as it is more casual to pick up your sketchbook while sipping a coffee and it gives you a distraction should you need one. Sketchbooks can be very small and you are unlikely to draw attention to yourself.

I spent some time in this café, sketching my croissant and coffee, the marble table top and the café's interior. Using a water-soluble pencil meant I could gently tease the line out with water to create a very light wash and the softness of the pencil on textured watercolour paper emphasized the tones. I concentrated on the 'still life' on the table and struggled with the view of the bar and chairs, stressing the diminishing size of the bars stools (see Perspective, pages 40–41). The few figures were a very small selection from the people in the café and they were in quite simple positions – the next section deals in more detail with including figures.

Once you get used to the idea of sketching in public, there are historic houses, museums, stations and architectural follies to explore, as well as restaurants, bars and pubs.

Including figures

Once outside the home, people will unavoidably be part of the interior scene. The trick is not to see them as separate but as shapes like anything else. The same sketching vocabulary – form, tone, scale and proportion – is needed, but the difference is that they move.

You will need to be swift and very selective. Avoid faces full one, avoid putting in too much detail and concentrate on conveying the essentials. People talking, drinking or eating, especially if sitting, will be absorbed and relatively still.

Remember that your focus is the interior; the presence of people is as natural as that of the furniture made to accommodate them and you would not capture the ambience of a café or bar if you were to sketch it empty.

The sketch made in the pub was in brush and grey watercolour over an underlying preliminary sketch in very loose pencil. The interior was authentic Edwardian and lighting was low key, the main source coming from the windows. Backlighting like this, known as 'contre-jour', throws figures into semi-silhouette, sometimes revealing little points, or rims, of light. This type of lighting has the advantage of letting you see the whole shape without too much distracting detail.

This pure like sketch, in fine fibre-tipped pen,
was done in a bit of a hurry for obvious reasons
– the boy was doing his homework and might
finish and leap up at any moment. I liked the
jumpers on the backs of the chairs. Stick to the
absolute minimum for a sketch like this: any less
would have been inadequate but more would
have looked less spontaneous.

154

Another line sketch, this time in pencil. Sewing is an excellent activity to catch for a sketch because it is inactive and time-consuming. The buildings through the window were reduced down to a mesh of lines. Take away the figure and something feels missing – but see page 159.

The sketch of the boy with the bowl of fruit is also done in pencil, but a very soft one, the heavy shading a mesh of lines in all directions. I used this technique as the room was very sombre (it was winter). I kept my hand moving constantly all over the place, building up the dark areas densely.

The charcoal pencil sketch in the kitchen is a little crude because of the speed necessary. It is a very domestic scene, dustbin included, and I am very grateful to the family for letting me sketch them looking so natural.

Looking out, looking in

Glimpses of views through a room into adjacent spaces can give depth and interest to a sketch.

The view of the street beyond the cat on the table, made in brush and paint, is very humble and really accidental as far as the cat is concerned. I think the curved shapes and the choice of this corner had just the right balance of detail and simplicity.

Looking out of the french windows on to the terrace I noticed that my wellington boots, walking shoes, dustbin and the plants combined in an interesting chance scene. I used pen and ink for a line sketch that concentrated on the contours of the items.

The sewing machine reappears, but this time I am more interested in the scene outside and the patterns of light. A carefully modulated wash over pencil depicted the slight changes of tone.

159

Multiple themes

A sketch will often be an interesting exercise in more than one way. The following combine several themes and are about bringing together the various ideas explored in this book.

The two sketches of my living room were approached differently and from slightly altered viewpoints. Looking at the same scene several times is very educational; you are bound to recognize pitfalls and improve on previous sketches. The scratchier version was sketched sitting and for a simpler image I stood but moved near the centre of the room. I took a great deal of artistic licence with the shelves and ultimately think that less information makes a better composition. Doing these two sketches taught me a lot.

Part 3
Sketching Landscapes

Keeping a sketchbook

As soon as I open one of my sketchbooks memories return of time spent in concentrated looking, contemplating and experiencing. I can feel the heat, cold, discomfort, excitement, atmosphere; even recall some dialogue, sounds, or reactions to my surroundings, thanks to scribbled notes in the margins. Time passes so quickly and my pile of books has grown, but sorting through them for this book has been reassuring justification for my obsessive practice of always keeping one on the go.

No artist's work will improve without observation, experimentation, risking failure. It's a personal quest which each individual has to undertake in their own way. A lot of this can be explored in a sketchbook and I would like to encourage you to begin one straight away if you haven't already done so. Only you can get the ball rolling. Start by keeping it like a private and personal diary until you gain confidence in your abilities. Other people's comments on your efforts can be inhibiting even if well meaning.

Pencil drawing of an ivy-clad tree stump. Here the foliage has been indicated by simple light and dark areas of tonal 'shading' with no attempt to show details of individual leaves.

Your personality will play a large part in the selection of your book; its size, shape, binding and paper. Many other factors come into play, and that's really what this book is all about.

I aim to share with you some practical experience developed through many years of pursuing this delightful activity and hope that you get as much joy from it as I do myself.

Pen and watercolour wash sketch on a windy morning, drawn across two pages of a sketchbook. In such conditions it's a good a good idea to carry paper clips or elastic bands in case you need to hold your pages down.

A visual diary

An extension of the use of a sketchbook may be to combine drawings, written notes, photos, collected tickets, cuttings, postcards, pressed flowers, feathers, seeds, scraps of fabric, colour samples; in short anything which can be stuck in a book to record your experiences or be useful reference material. Some sketches can be done on the spot, but if you train your visual memory you can draw things later from your 'memory banks'. The more you draw from observation the better your visual recall will become.

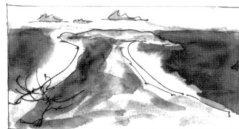

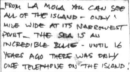

Visual research

For the serious student or practitioner of art and design, visual research is a way of collecting relevant information in relation to a set of needs. An illustration may need to include historically accurate details, for example, so a visit to a museum or library equipped with a trusty sketchbook might be an obvious starting point.

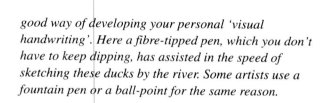

Pencil study of a tree trunk. Interesting subjects are all around us. The act of focusing attention and attempting a sketch will help to reveal them once we start making marks on paper. Artists call this 'seeing through drawing'.

Rapid pen sketches trying to capture gestures rather than detail. Drawing directly with a pen without preliminary pencil work forces you to sum up a situation in the simplest terms. If a line is wrong you have to 'overdraw' the first mark because it is impossible to rub out. This is a good way of developing your personal 'visual handwriting'. Here a fibre-tipped pen, which you don't have to keep dipping, has assisted in the speed of sketching these ducks by the river. Some artists use a fountain pen or a ball-point for the same reason.

Designers frequently collect together sources of inspiration to assist in the generation of new ideas. For the landscape artist the sketchbook can be a way of collecting visual information which may later be put together in more finished compositions. Figures, animals, plants or buildings can be introduced to enliven a painting done indoors in studio conditions.

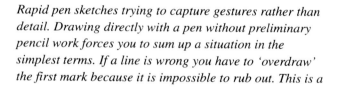

Pen line and wash. Animals keep on the move but you have to make a start drawing them. Try to retain a visual memory and hope that they will oblige you with a fresh chance to finish your sketch at a later stage; they tend to resume the same pose every so often. A camera will help if you run short of time.

Basic tools

A bewildering variety of drawing implements is now available but it is best to start with the most basic ones and get to know what effects they can produce. Sketching outdoors requires that you travel light, carrying only a small selection of tried and trusted tools and equipment.

Pencils, crayons, pastels and charcoal

To some extent your choice of these will influence your approach, direct what you look at and the information you are able to put down in a sketch. In general hard (H) grade pencils or sharp pointed implements such as pens, drawn on smooth paper surfaces make it possible to record fine details, whereas soft (B) grade pencils, charcoal, crayons or pastels drawn on to rough-surfaced papers are best for broad tonal impressions – such as the sketch top right.

Soft pencils will become blunt quickly so it is important to have a craft knife or a sharpener handy. Another vital tool is a kneadable eraser which can be moulded to a point to help clean up, lighten areas, or pick out highlights without smudging. You can blend tones with your fingers or specially made rolled cardboard torchons. It is probably a good idea to spray such drawings with fixative if you don't want a messy sketchbook.

Soft pencil drawing on cartridge paper showing general distribution of light and dark tones.

Chalk pastel sketch on rough textured paper, which enables a quick, bold treatment.

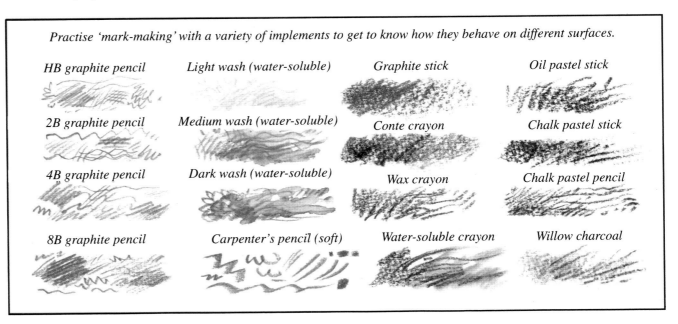

Practise 'mark-making' with a variety of implements to get to know how they behave on different surfaces.

HB graphite pencil Light wash (water-soluble) Graphite stick Oil pastel stick

2B graphite pencil Medium wash (water-soluble) Conte crayon Chalk pastel stick

4B graphite pencil Dark wash (water-soluble) Wax crayon Chalk pastel pencil

8B graphite pencil Carpenter's pencil (soft) Water-soluble crayon Willow charcoal

Felt tips, fibre tips

With so many new products on the market it is worthwhile experimenting to find which felt tips or fibre tips suit your requirements. Some are water resistant, which is important to test if you intend to put a wash over them. Others bleed through the paper, appearing on the reverse side of the sheet or, worse still, going through several layers. The pigments used may also fade after a while if exposed to daylight. However, they are cheap, portable and a great asset for quick sketching.

Rollerballs, brushpens, fine liners, technical and calligraphy pens all provide the artist with different qualities of line.

Pens, ink and brushes

More traditional dip pens are capable of great flexibility and variety of marks. Usually they are dipped into inks which are either 'fixed' or waterproof when dry, or unfixed, which are not, but have the qualities of making very good washes without clogging up pens or brushes.

Reed pens, bamboo pens and quills can be cut, sharpened and customized to suit your needs.

Steel nibs, which can be fitted into holders, come in a variety of widths and can give varied line widths depending on the pressure you apply.

Fountain pens for sketching are useful but must usually be used with unfixed ink.

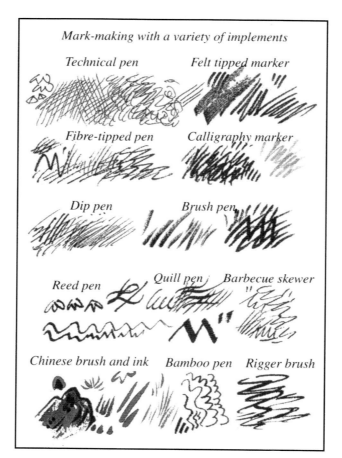

Chinese ink sticks, ground with water on small stone pallets, can be modified in strength from the palest to richest blacks depending on the fineness of the grinding. In conjunction with Chinese brushes these enable wonderfully expressive effects.

Sable and synthetic hair brushes are also available in a wide variety sizes and forms. A 'rigger', a brush with long hair used by nautical painters to draw in the fine lines of rigging, can be almost like a pencil to draw with.

Pen sketch on smooth paper. Tones have to be made by cross-hatched lines.

Line and wash sketch on watercolour paper. Begun with a water-resistant fibre-tipped pen, the tonal ink washes were applied afterwards with a sable brush.

Paper surfaces

There is a wide range of sketchbooks to choose from, ranging from low-cost cartridge pads to expensive, hand-made and bound watercolour books. You can, of course, use a drawing board and individual sheets of paper and vary the surfaces to suit each situation and purpose.

In general there are three types of paper surface:
• smooth or 'hot pressed' (mechanically pressed through hot rollers) which is suitable for fine detail and pen work;
• semi-rough or 'not pressed' which will suit most purposes;
• rough and textured papers which suit broader treatments.

Other important factors are the thickness or weight of the paper and its absorbency, which will affect its suitability for wash treatments if you wish to use them. You are generally safe with a sketchbook designated for watercolour, or if you buy heavier weight papers. Cheaper lightweight papers need to be 'stretched' on a drawing board as they tend to buckle when water is applied to them.

To stretch paper, wet the sheet thoroughly so that it goes floppy and attach it firmly to a board with brown gumstrip parcel tape around all the edges. When the paper dries it should stretch taut again and not buckle too much when water-colour washes are applied.

Pen sketch on smooth hot pressed paper. Ideal for quick line drawing in pen or harder grade pencils.

Brush drawing on semi-rough watercolour paper without preliminary pencil work.

Pencil on inexpensive cartridge paper. The smooth surface is ideal for general drawing and detailed work.

Pen line and wash sketch on watercolour paper. A pen draws the linework first; loose washes are then applied.

Subject matter

It is tempting to go in search of great imposing vistas to sketch in the manner of the landscapes displayed in national galleries. The trouble is that this could involve long journeys out of your home territory, crowds of sightseers and eventual frustration at your failure to do justice to the scene.

Often really worthwhile subjects are right under our noses waiting to be discovered. An old tree or a broken gate could be much more manageable to start with. Even with the most mundane of subjects, other qualities somehow seem to emerge as we get into looking closely and trying to represent what we see. Time spent in looking before drawing is seldom wasted.

In the scene above, I liked the way the three trees seemed to lean towards each other as if in conversation.

Everyday subjects can become more interesting as you begin to draw them. Imperfections like the broken fence of this derelict cottage made me want to do this pencil sketch. The bird obligingly perched on the fence just long enough to be included. A short time afterwards the site was redeveloped and the garden smartened up. The landscape is in a constant state of change and a drawing can be a unique historical record.

Drawing shouldn't be a tedious activity; if you get bored just leave out things you don't find interesting. Bring in other elements you want to include or move them about to add to your composition – drawing should be a reflection of your personality.

Pen sketch on smooth cartridge paper which began with a study of exposed tree roots. Subjects like this are good practice and readily available if you seek them out.

A simple subject: the path of a small stream in the corner of a field. It was drawn on to smooth cartridge paper with charcoal pencils, which can be sharpened to give a precise black line or smudged to give broader areas of tone.

Try looking for arrangements of light and dark tones which you can see more easily by squinting at your subject through half-closed eyes. Don't be afraid to leave white space in your drawing. The balance of positive and negative areas brings vitality to a composition. Cut a small window out of a piece of card to act as a viewfinder if you have problems in selecting what to focus on.

The sketch on the right was drawn with a soft (3B) graphite pencil on smooth cartridge paper. This was once the entrance to an old country mansion and the tonal arrangements and rhythms of the branches interested me. A few months later the ball had fallen off its plinth and work begun to convert the house into luxury apartments.

Simple perspective

As you progress with the art of drawing a sense of perspective becomes more instinctive but initially creating a sense of distance can be a stumbling block and rather off-putting. Creating an illusion of depth and recession is achieved in landscape sketching by establishing a contrast between foreground, middle ground and distance. Our judgement of distance is prompted by various visual clues which could be represented in a sketch.

Our eye level establishes a horizon which is apparent when we look out to sea, but when we look at a landscape it is usually less obvious.

Details appear larger and more distinct in the foreground and the further away things are, the fainter and less defined they become. This effect, termed 'aerial perspective', can be usefully emphasized by making a distinct tonal contrast between the foreground and background layers of a landscape drawing.

Other helpful visual clues include overlapping areas, forms and contours, which define whether one thing is in front of another, and making the intervals between similar sized elements such as furrows on ploughed fields or ripples on water appear to diminish in size as they recede in the distance.

Where we position the horizon line on a page creates a subdivision between the areas of land and sky. Dynamic compositions can be achieved by allowing one or the other to dominate, rather than making everything symmetrical.

Your viewpoint should reflect the focus of your interests. If, for example, you wish to make a feature of the sky or look down on a scene, make the horizon lower down on your page.

If you are more interested in the foreground make the horizon higher up.

Once the eye level has been established in a sketch, all structures or elements in the landscape have to be drawn in relationship to it if we wish them to be 'in perspective'.

ONE POINT PERSPECTIVE

VP

HORIZON

Generally all receding parallel lines above your eye level appear to slant down towards the horizon and those below your eye level appear to travel upward. These converge on a point commonly known as a vanishing point (**VP**). '**One point perspective**' as illustrated above, is a term used to describe this type of viewpoint when there may be only one obvious vanishing point.

As an experiment, try securing some tracing paper over a photograph of some buildings and, using a ruler, trace lines which seem to converge to see where they intersect. From this you can deduce the camera level and the point at which the lens was focused.

TWO POINT PERSPECTIVE

VP 1   focal point of the camera lens   VP 2

When you face a building corner-on, with its sides receding away acutely on either side, there will be two sets of vanishing points, one to the left and the other to the right. This is commonly known as '**two point perspective**'.

Tones and shapes

The forms and textures of the landscape are revealed to us by light; but since this varies throughout the day and is modified by weather conditions, we are frequently struggling to capture fleeting effects.

Spend time studying how light falling on objects or the landscape affects a view – shadows cast in strong sunlight can give us hard-edged shapes, whereas more diffused lighting will be soft and atmospheric. Exploit the contrasts between light and dark areas in your drawing and indicate any big shapes first before getting involved in any detail.

'Form' is a term used to describe the visual appearance and shape of something. Methods of representing form can be by the use of line and 'tones' (a range of values from light to dark). We can help to create an impression of solidity by adding tones, as in the part-completed demonstration above.

Techniques of 'modelling' using tones depend on the medium you choose. Soft media, such as pastel, charcoal, crayon or graphite, as shown on the left, enable you to lay down large areas of tonal shading. With a hard pen, however, you have to render tones by cross-hatched lines or stippling, as shown below.

Skies and clouds

When there are no clouds in the sky it can be represented by a gentle gradation of tone; palest near the horizon and darkening towards the top. The appearance of clouds, however, is greatly influenced by the direction and elevation of the sun or moon. They are usually on the move so we have to work rapidly in appropriate media in order to capture the transient effects.

You don't have to travel to do sky studies. It's possible to do them looking out of a window, although being out of doors has a special quality, especially in flat country where the skies seem to dominate the landscape.

The diagram on the left attempts to show how clouds in their own way conform to perspective, and how the prevailing direction of the sun can light some areas whilst throwing other parts into shadow.

Small 'on-the-spot' sketches such as these try to capture the effects of rapidly moving clouds and contrasting lighting conditions. Some are done with soft pencils and others make use of directly applied watercolour washes.

Mountains and hills

From a high viewpoint you are able to watch the interplay of light crossing the landscape and revealing the basic topological structures below. Buildings, roads, rivers, lakes, hedgerows and trees are all part of the rich vocabulary of forms which can be included in our sketches.

It is helpful for our sense of tranquillity, self-importance and relativity to see small figures and cars dwarfed within expanses of space. Whether looking down from a height or up towards a mountain it gives us an impression of our own fragile and transitory nature.

The crayon sketch below was done across two pages of a sketchbook like using a wide-angled lens on a camera. Gliders were catching the thermals off the Downs in afternoon sunshine. It is fun to include figures, if they turn up, to add a feeling of scale and human interest.

Water

In its many forms water plays a vital part in shaping the landscape and is a great subject for study. After rain the glistening reflections in puddles or on road surfaces can totally transform and enliven a foreground. Reflections are not simply a reverse image of a subject but can reveal its underside. They usually appear lighter than dark objects being reflected and darker than light objects.

It is rare to get a perfect mirrored surface and usually some disturbance distorts the reflection, presenting the artist with a challenge to render the moving patterns produced. Practise using various tools to capture these, for example a rigger brush or a calligraphy pen.

Rapidly moving or agitated water has to be suggested since we can't draw its detail without freezing its motion. The charcoal pencil sketch on the left traces the path of a stream down through some rocks. It was an exercise in leaving things out and was influenced by the book on Chinese painting which I was reading that day.

Rigger brush marks   *Calligraphy pen marks*

Rocks and cliffs

Geological formations offer good opportunities for study and lend themselves to rendering with most media. It is awe-inspiring to contemplate the massive forces and upheavals which have taken place to generate such forms.

The rhythmic layering of sedimentary rocks, rich textures or smooth worn surfaces present qualities which provide interesting subject matter. Changes of light throughout the day can also reveal different aspects while we sketch.

I like to observe the way people come and go like actors against an enduring backdrop. Some have been included in the pen and crayon sketch below to give a sense of scale and contrast against the sea-hewn rock formations.

Lulworth Cove. 25th July

Trees

All trees have definite structures which can best be seen during winter, before they are obscured with masses of leaves. Apart from each species having its own distinctive shape they acquire a character shaped by age and environment. Studies of bare trees enable us to observe bark textures and rhythms of growth.

Sketches with pen or pencil should attempt to simplify detail and emphasize these qualities, starting with the major trunk and branches before tapering off towards a suggestion of the finer twigs.

Even when clothed in foliage it is important to visualize the underlying structure of a tree in order to draw or paint it convincingly. Look for the main massing of leaves and distribution of areas of shadow, retaining some patches of light which break through the cover and emphasize branches where they stand out against foliage or the sky. Rendering leaf textures requires a form of visual shorthand which you develop with practice. It is good to simplify where possible.

I find it beautiful to consider elements in the landscape having relationships and spiritual qualities. An ancient book on Chinese painting refers to 'old trees with grave dignity and an air of compassion, leading by the hand modest and retiring young trees'. Sketching outdoors can become a bit like meditation, and very uplifting providing you can overcome some of the occasional discomforts.

This rapid line and wash sketch was done whilst sitting comfortably on a convenient stile. However, an inflatable air cushion is easy to transport and adds a touch of luxury on some occasions.

Cottages and villages

Much of the regional character of our landscape is the result of buildings constructed from local materials, using traditional architecture. The pen sketch on the right is a shorthand note of the basic soft organic shapes of timber-framed cottages against contrasting tree forms.

Frequently, modernization of buildings in towns and villages smartens up their fronts but leaves the backs or rooflines comparatively untouched. It's possible to find some interesting subjects behind the facades: abandoned stables, sheds or relics of the past, like the old pump in the wash drawing below.

By visualizing the possible effects of light coming from the left, this original line sketch was later used to develop the more finished tonal drawing below.

Ancient buildings

Old buildings offer rich areas of exploration. Apart from a study of architecture and the possible challenges of perspective there are usually opportunities to discover textures and small details which might be less obvious but more interesting to draw. Attempting to render surfaces with different media can also be very rewarding.

The freehand drawing on the right was done with a dip-in pen and without the use of a ruler, to give it character and avoid making it look too mechanical. A wax crayon was used as a resist to help create stone textures before an ink wash was applied. Small natural sponges dipped into paint or ink can also be effective.

Rendering of stone surface textures using a sponge.

A line drawing for reproduction at different scales, using a technical pen.

The industrial landscape

In contrast to more conventionally picturesque rural landscapes, the marks of industry can make dramatic and fascinating subjects. A building site, quarry, power station or dock, for example, can be teeming with interest.

The sketch below was done standing up looking through a gap in the protective fencing surrounding a building site. A chill wind was blowing at the time and the discomfort definitely speeded up my pen.

It's a good idea to draw in the basic immovable components before adding figures and vehicles which come and go. This is now a local shopping centre and an example of recording 'history in the making'.

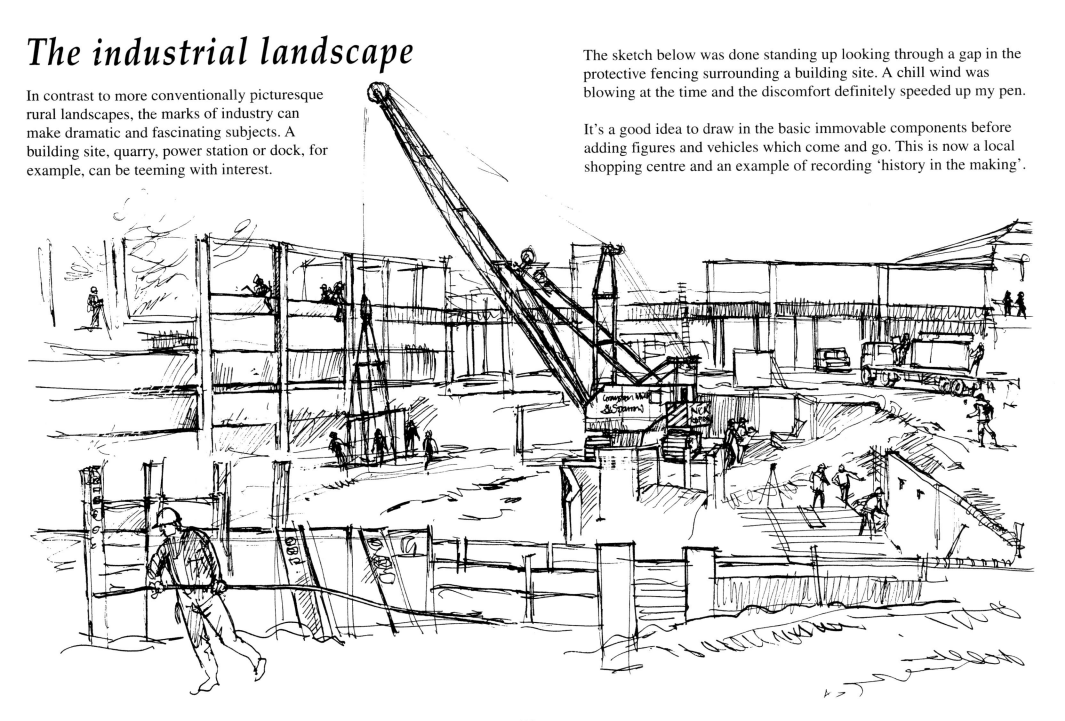

Farm buildings and equipment

Seldom pre-planned and usually built and maintained for purely functional purposes, collections of farm buildings are great to draw. Their strong shapes and structures, contrasting surface textures and materials all reflect constant changes of agricultural technology. Redundant equipment or derelict buildings are other favourite subjects and can create a ghost-town atmosphere, as the sketches on the next two pages show.

From a quick shorthand outline drawing such as this one above, it is possible to develop a more solid tonal rendering as shown below by establishing the direction of sunlight and emphasizing the contrasting shadows.

Fields, hedges, walls and gates

There's a great variety of subject matter to be found in this theme – an air of mystery about tunnels through overhanging branches leading to unknown vistas; weathered and worn old gates each with their own history.

In the sketch above, I was experimenting using a white wax crayon as a resist so that highlights were created in the darker overlying watercolour washes.

It can be a bit fussy and difficult to control because once you put the wax on you are stuck with it even if you don't like the effect.

However, the best way of finding new treatments is to risk making mistakes.

Country lanes

I'll admit a great affection for little, drunkenly winding lanes, away from the motorways. You never know what's round the bend, and if on foot you have a chance to hear the birds or the scurry of the odd fieldmouse or weasel in the undergrowth. Varieties of plants and insects, the changing seasons, passing joggers, people on horseback; all make walking a very different experience, and reveal a lot of things to sketch.

Seasons of the year

There are times of the year when working outdoors is a really pleasant occupation but weather conditions are not always favourable. Some of my sketches have been done in lay-bys, viewed through a car windscreen with rain or snow falling outside and a camera handy to capture fleeting breaks in the cloud. Despite the adverse conditions, the winter months are a good time to see the landscape stripped bare or simplified by snow.

The watercolour below was done using Chinese brushes which are very good for broad washes. With only a little paint or pigment on the brush, the hairs can also be split to produce interesting dry brushmarks.

The bare tree and stile above were drawn using a flexible handmade quill pen, loaded with watercolour to give a sensitive line even on rough paper. Washes were then applied to fill in the larger areas of tone.

CUTTING A REED OR A QUILL PEN

Make a long scoop cut at the end.   *Shape the nib shoulders.*   *On a firm surface trim the end,*   *and make a little slit.*

Pare down the inside to make it flat.   *For a finer pen trim the upper edge of the nib.*   *Load with watercolour or ink; turn over to use.*

The same stile and tree as the previous page, but painted in summer, when lots of foliage and undergrowth make it hard to recognize as the same place. Here a brush has been used directly to lay simple washes, forming edges by the contrast in tones rather than relying on drawn outlines to define them.

Harvest time has been revolutionized by technology and although the fields are not perhaps as visually attractive as the haystacks painted by Monet, I keep telling myself to look for beauty in this present day and age rather than dwelling on nostalgia.

WORKING WITH A REED OR QUILL PEN

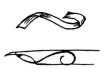

As an optional extra a reservoir can be added to your pen by cutting a thin slither of flexible plastic or metal. Bend it into an S shape and insert into the barrel of the nib a little short of the tip. The S shape holds the reservoir in place and should feed ink down more gradually rather than causing blots. You may remove it for cleaning purposes.

Loading the nib with a brush is more effective than dipping into an ink bottle and you can also use watercolour by scraping the nib across a brush held in your other hand. This enables you to draw fine lines and details in a watercolour with precision and to use pigments at different strengths.

189

Changing light and atmosphere

Changing lighting conditions radically alter the landscape by picking out some features or throwing others into obscurity. No matter how fast we work these effects can be quite fleeting and create very different moods. Sometimes a camera is the only way to capture them, or to return at the same time of day hoping for similar conditions, but there are times when we have to rely on visual memory.

Sketching at speed

Drawing at speed obviously dictates the amount of detail and information that can be included. This is not always a disadvantage since it helps to develop a form of visual shorthand, rather like our personal handwriting, with excitement and energy in the marks.

Setting time limits and moving on to new situations is a good exercise in training the hand and eye to sum up essentials.

These sketches were done whilst standing up, using a fibre-tipped pen without any preliminary pencil drawing.

The camera as back-up

When sketching we focus our attention on visual qualities and open up our perceptions so that the whole act becomes a unique and memorable experience. Perhaps time or circumstances require us to move on before we finish the work or we want to continue or develop it elsewhere. A camera can be used as an extension to the sketchbook for gathering information.

Even with a wide-angle lens it may not be possible to include all that you would like in one shot, so several can be patched together to create a panorama. It is so much better working from your own photographic reference since it relates to your own perception and motivation rather than copying another's viewpoint.

Close-ups of details such as plants or rocks, or transitory moving elements such as people or animals, can all be brought together to improve a composition. There is a value in compiling your own system of reference photographs which can be accessed when needed. Mine are kept in shoeboxes divided into categories such as 'skies', 'boats', 'wild flowers', or 'farm animals', for example, or vaguer notions such as 'textures' or 'light effects'. A collection like this soon grows and this rough and ready filing system at least saves me from having to scrabble through the whole collection every time I need inspiration or reference.

Travels with a sketchbook

It's more challenging than a camera but wonderfully satisfying to record your travelling experiences in a sketchbook. Try to be as inconspicuous as possible since people can be very curious or even resentful of this strange activity. A minimal kit of equipment which can fit into a pocket or a small bag is ideal. At times I pretend to be writing a postcard which tends to look a bit private and less likely to attract attention.

ΠΑΝΤΟΠΩΛΕΙΟ 'MARKET'

Saturday 8th July
Drinking Lemonade +
Greek Coffee - after beach
View from Café

windmill

sun Beach 19 july

Yakikavak

monday 27 June

Avilas - Corfu

Sat 21 July

Composition

To draw things together in a pictorial composition we may incorporate images compiled from a variety of sources. Sketchbook drawings or photographs, for example, or magazine cuttings may just be helpful in triggering off a mood, a memory or an association, rather than being slavishly copied.

This composition was put together from several sources. The guinea fowl were from separate photographs taken in the same location as the old barn; the background and figures were then added from imagination.

Pictorial composition involves control and manipulation of elements within a design area. We may try to do this in a sketch by adjusting the viewpoint, moving something or even leaving it out (something a photograph can't do). Below are some useful principles.

Compositions can be organized according to 'the rule of thirds', by which imaginary lines divide the picture area into thirds both horizontally and vertically. Strong elements can coincide with these lines.

The principle of balancing overlapping areas, forms and contours is the basis of all pictorial creation. Since line is our first means of defining these, then linear arrangement becomes our first consideration.

It is helpful to try out some simple thumbnail sketches like these illustrated, where the arrangement of major forms to be included is explored and adjusted before embarking on a full-scale layout.

Every good picture should have a main focal point. All lines should draw the eye towards that spot and an imaginary horizontal and vertical should cross at the main point of interest within the composition.

The sketch below has some strong diagonals made by the structure of the gate, leading the eye towards the small cart which was the focal point. This was done on the spot but follows the 'rule of thirds' quite instinctively.

Many successful compositions can be based on simple implied geometrical shapes such as triangles or circles.

In every good picture there should be a planned easy and natural path for the eye to travel. You can make the eye follow a given course by use of line. Lead the eye in, entertain it with a spot of interest and then allow it to pass out of the composition. It should be a pleasing path and not obstructed or given two ways to go. The eye should enter at the bottom and emerge at the top rather than at the sides. Lines leading out of the subject should be stopped by some device or another line leading back to the focal point.

The sketch above was done looking through a car windscreen on a chilly afternoon. It becomes a challenge to find a good parking space with a view that doesn't obstruct passing traffic!

The painting on the right is based on this sketch but with a change of format from vertical to horizontal. To attempt to make it look like one of the early railway posters which first inspired me to take up landscape painting I have used opaque poster paints. These allow tones to be overpainted and rendered in a simplified, flat manner.

Landscapes with figures

Paintings without people in them can seem to lack interest; when they are included a sort of empathy enables us in some way to enter the picture. Figures can therefore act as potent elements within a pictorial composition.

A consideration of composition is essential to successful painting. Without a good underlying structure the whole thing can fail to hang together, and no clever technique or style can save it. Good composition involves the careful placing of, and fitting together of, all the elements in the picture. If we study and analyse the work of many past and contemporary painters, we can observe how carefully their work has been composed. Try laying a piece of tracing paper over a postcard or reproduction, and then trace the major subdivisions and lines of sight which the artist has used. Notice how, in some, the placing of a figure or group of figures, animals or human artefacts has been used to good effect. Imagine what the picture would have been like without them.

It is sometimes not necessary to make figures too sharply defined or identifiable. They can be simply strategically placed blobs of paint, shapes, flicks of colour; more like impressions of a presence than a detailed description of a male or female figure wearing any specific type of clothing or performing any particular function. This is most appropriate when the rest of the painting is equally simplified.

However, when we move to more detailed paintings other factors have to be considered, such as perspective, gesture and shape. And what are the figures doing? Age, gender and clothing, as well as interrelationships and accessories, have to be described. These are not easy to suggest without observation, experience and practice. This is again where keeping, and constantly using, a sketchbook is particularly vital to the figurative artist.

The above pen line drawing intended for reproduction in a magazine includes ducks, geese and figures on horseback added to compile an impression of a particular location.

You can 'hang' your figures on the horizon line by making it cut through similar figures in the same place. This keeps them on the same ground plane.

The wash and crayon sketch above could be developed into a composition with added human interest by perhaps including someone walking a dog, wheeling a bicycle or riding a horse, like these examples found in some of my other sketchbooks. The thumbnail layout on the left shows how a figure could fit into the composition.

Composing a picture

This page demonstrates how to assemble a composition from a variety of sources.

The pen sketch on the right has some written comments to point out important features and notes to assist in the use of colour if it is going to be used at a later stage.

To back this up I took various panoramic photographs, including trees to the right of the road which threw long shadows at a certain time of the afternoon.

I searched for some possible human interest to introduce and did thumbnail layouts to find a suitable location within the composition, which appears in its final form on the opposite page.

Part 4
Sketching Harbours and Boats

Preparation

Everyone's personal preference in choice of materials and methods will be different. Like many other pursuits, we only discover the way of working that is most comfortable for us by trying different things. In the context of this particular book I felt it was important not to offer too wide a range of options because that can be a little perplexing.

When I was at secondary school I can well remember, despite the cajoling of my enthusiastic art master, how confident I felt with a pencil in my hand and how unconvincing were my efforts in other media – I was particularly terrified of oil paints. In my opinion, graphite pencils are the most versatile and forgiving of all mark-making tools, and probably the most underrated in terms of artistic results.

For this reason, I have put the emphasis in this book firmly on pencil work whilst suggesting just a few interesting variations and alternatives which I feel offer a natural progression once the basic skills have been mastered.

Choosing pencils

Were you to walk into a local newsagent and ask to buy a pencil, you would undoubtedly be sold an HB, the most common grade which lies about halfway along the scale between soft and hard.

Although they are sometimes useful for lightly sketching in outlines before getting down to the real business of drawing, HBs are really neither fish nor fowl – not hard enough for precise lines and at the same time not soft enough to produce a good tonal range.

As a rough guide, look at the range of marks on the right made by the points of ordinary graphite pencils. See how the point of the very hardest pencil, the 8H, produces a thin, light grey line which barely varies in width or tone, no matter how hard you press down on it.

The 6B, at the other end of the scale, is a more versatile tool, particularly useful for broad tonal areas of gradations from light to dark. Different amounts of pressure on the tip give you varying depths of tone.

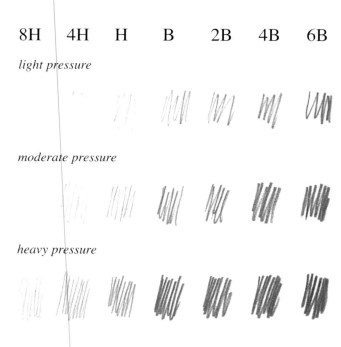

| 8H | 4H | H | B | 2B | 4B | 6B |

light pressure

moderate pressure

heavy pressure

Ultimately you will find your own favourite range of pencils but, if you start with two each of the above range, you will, through practice, get used to the characteristics of each type and find out for yourself which is most suited to the kind of sketching you want to do.

HB sketch.

The Astral, moored in the commercial port at Dubrovnik, Croatia.

As a general rule, I tend to use hard pencils, and sometimes a ruler as well, on smooth, or 'hot-press', paper to deal with complicated or very find detail, like the rigging of the schooner on this page. Notice how the harder lead gives a virtually uniform weight of line. Softer pencils at this sort of scale would not give a precise enough line to pick out the detail clearly.

The only other way to convey the whole of a subject like this with a 'blacker' or more varied mark would be to alter the scale, i.e. draw it bigger on a much larger sheet of paper. This would obviously be very cumbersome and probably take far too long, particularly if you're perched on a bollard on the dockside, as I was.

The better alternative, I always find, is to get up close, to concentrate on just a small area of the subject as in these other two drawings, both done with a 4B pencil on smooth heavyweight cartridge paper.

H

2B

6B

Tonal effects with pencils

To create areas of tone in different shades of grey there are a number of options. Any pencil, sharpened with a blade or a rotary sharpener (I always use a surgical scalpel with inter-changeable, 10A blades), will give a broader and lighter mark when the side of the lead is held almost flat on the paper.

The width and tonal strength of the mark is usually determined by the softness of the lead. The very soft pencils with 'fat' leads can also be carefully fashioned with a sharp blade into a square, or chiselled, end. On the left are some examples of tonal effects achieved with different kinds of leads.

Using the side of the lead, or the chiselled end, of a very soft pencil on a lightly-abraded surface allows you to fill large areas of more or less uniform tone ranging from light grey to almost black. At the same time, using the sharpened point of the same pencil allows you to produce the dark, hard edges required, for instance, to define the jibs of the cranes in the 4B drawing on the right. Four distinct tonal areas are here achieved with varying pressures on the side of the same lead.

Hatching and crosshatching are ways of building flat or graduated areas of tone. With hatching, all the strokes go in the same direction; with crosshatching, they go in different directions and are overlaid – one hatched area on top of

another. These two techniques have the advantage of blending with the outlines of objects and are particularly suitable when you need to keep the key, or overall tone, of the drawing light and open.

Choice of paper

Unlike media such as oil paints or watercolours, you can by and large draw with pencil on almost any surface. There are, however, some papers which are designed to receive pencil more sympathetically than others.

In order not to complicate matters I tend to see it as a straightforward choice between three simple options:

- Smooth cartridge or hot-press paper of varying weights for general purpose sketching and for detailed work. You can use almost any kind of media on this surface, with the notable exception of oil-based paints. It is advisable, however, that you use a heavier weight, say 220gsm, if you want to apply a wash to your drawing – otherwise it will tend to stretch and 'cockle'. A3 or A4 size pads are widely available.

- Lightly-abraded, more absorbent surfaces, such as Not or CS2, for looser more textured results, including line and wash or the use of water-soluble pencils. This can be virtually any weight as the surface is designed to be very versatile and won't distort. Colour-tinted surfaces, such as Canson paper, are also quite popular, particularly for charcoal, crayon or pastel work.

- Pre-stretched watercolour papers for acrylics, gouache or watercolours. My personal favourite is called Arches, but it is rather expensive and doesn't come in pads. There are two or three well-known and perfectly good brands that are reasonably priced and widely available in pads of various sizes.

The sketches above and to the right show the application of different methods of hatching. The seagull hovering on an updraft was done with an H pencil and the aft-deck of the racing yacht was drawn with a 4B pencil.

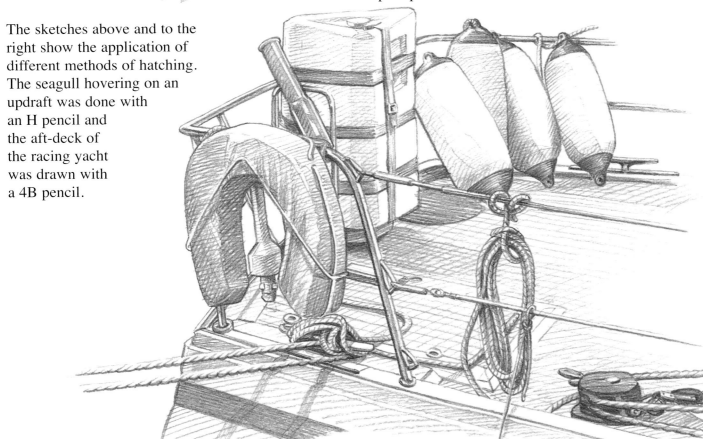

Of course you do not have to stick to these guidelines and, no doubt, as you progress you will, through experimentation, find papers and boards which more particularly suit your technique.

On this page and the opposite one are some examples of the effects that you can achieve drawing on these different types of paper in various media.

Other essentials

I have already mentioned the use of a surgical scalpel for sharpening pencils. A packet of emery boards or a small grindstone, made from fine sandpaper wrapped around a block of wood, are useful additions to the sketcher's armoury as they will help to keep your pencil points needle-sharp without you having continually to shave lumps off the wooden shaft.

Some artists prefer to use 'clutch pencils' with self-propelling and interchangeable leads. Personally, as I am generally quite heavy-handed, I find the leads in these more inclined to break than in the conventional type of pencil. Most of the people I know who use them are architects or industrial designers, using 2H or 3H leads for the light, precise lines required in measured drawings.

Line and was sketch on CS2 paper – a family inflating their dinghy at Salcombe, Devon.

2B pencil on smooth cartridge paper – a ten-minute sketch of the Old City port, Dubrovnik, Croatia.

There is a great deal of good sense and no shame in using an eraser to get rid of unwanted marks. There are two types which I use regularly. The first is a soft putty rubber which will gently expunge almost any pencil mark from any kind of surface, by transferring it onto the rubber. Pressing hard won't damage the paper surface but the eraser itself tends to get very dirty.

The other type is the much harder and more conventional type of pencil rubber. Whilst these are generally more effective in getting rid of errors on even the softest papers, they can damage the drawing surface if you rub too hard. I generally use a hard rubber only on very hard surfaces such as line boards or canvas.

A short ruler may come in handy, especially if you lack confidence with drawing straight, or 'straightish', lines freehand. Again, there is no shame whatsoever in using any mechanical aid that helps you to achieve the desired result.

If you intend to work with a ready-made proprietary pad of paper with a stiff card backing there is probably no need for a drawing board as well. However, it is occasionally difficult to hold steady the paper you're working on, particularly in a gusting wind, so a not-too-bendy piece of plywood or hardboard, no larger than A2 and not too thick (so it remains easy to carry), should do the trick.

Four large stainless steel drawing board clips from the art shop should be enough to secure the paper or pad onto the board unless you're planning to go sketching in a hurricane. On the subject of inclement weather, it's a good idea always to carry a large polythene or waterproof bag to protect your work and materials just in case you get caught out in the rain.

The final item I feel it worth mentioning in the sketcher's equipment list is a comfortable folding stool, preferably one with built-in pockets for all the other equipment you need. One of these need not be very costly and it will save having to carry a separate bag for your materials.

Gouache on Arches rough paper – Bill Hoskins on Chapel Porth beach, Cornwall.

Although I do own an artists' stool, I often leave it behind when I go sketching and, equally often, regret having done so as I find myself sitting for an hour or so on a patch of wet grass or a knobbly bit of concrete.

Watercolour sketch on Watman paper – yacht race at Salcombe, Devon.

Building confidence

In order to prepare yourself for a sketching session it is a good idea, especially if you are just beginning, to try a few simple drawing exercises. They will help you to get the feel of the process and to ensure that you feel comfortable with the materials you have chosen.

Assuming you are armed with a relatively soft pencil and a pad of smooth cartridge paper, try lightly running the point of the pencil horizontally across the sheet about 3cm down from the top and from left to right, or right to left if you're left-handed. The line will never be completely straight, regardless of whether you are an accomplished artist, but you will find that by resting the heel of your hand gently on the paper's surface, you will have more control.

Now try drawing a vertical line about 3cm in from the edge of the page. By hooking your little finger loosely onto the side of the pad and keeping it stiff as you move your hand downwards, the line will run parallel to the edge and be fairly straight. Try these two exercises a number of times with different grades of lead.

Next, look at the sketch on the left-hand side of page 204 and try to copy the different strengths of tone. Choose a pencil of equivalent softness to one of the three areas and get used to feeling the varying pressures and angles of the lead required to make these kind of marks.

The final exercise is called the *Drawing Race*. Take one sheet of paper only and, using the initial letter of your first name, try to draw ten objects which begin with the same letter within just five minutes.

If you've ever play *Pictionary*, you'll be familiar with the idea. The trick is to find the visual essence of the object and draw it as if you're trying to make yourself understood to someone who doesn't speak English. On the right is my attempt to represent ten objects beginning with the letter 'r'.

Having done these exercises you should feel a little better equipped to tackle that most terrifying of all things to an artist – the blank sheet of paper.

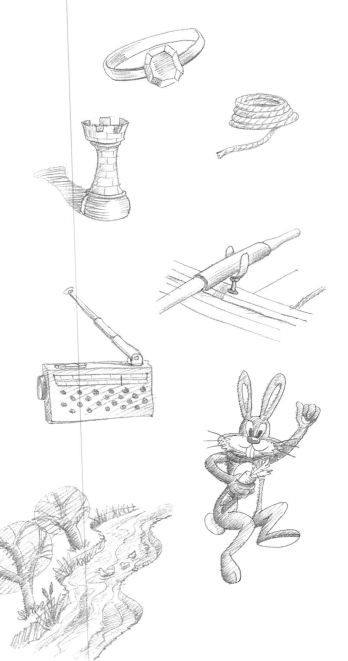

Choosing a subject

There is an old mnemonic in the world of advertising represented by the initials KISS. These stand for 'Keep It Simple, Stupid', a marvellous piece of advice for those starting sketching.

Given the enormous and diverse choice of interesting subjects available in, for example, a busy fishing port, it is always a great temptation to try and fill your picture with as much detailed information as possible.

A good way of avoiding the pitfalls of over-ambition when beginning is deliberately to select a small and well-defined group of objects that are not too far away from you. Try to find a line of vision which excludes a distant horizon and does not incorporate tall buildings, people or complex things.

Low tide at Barmouth, Gwynedd, Wales.

Fish boxes on the quay at Mousehole, Cornwall.

211

A few basic rules

Setting up

Finding the right spot to settle down for an hour or two is equally as important as choosing the right subjects.

Always try to ensure that what you are drawing is not going to change significantly before you've finished. It would be very frustrating to find that the boat which is the focal point of the intended picture suddenly weighs anchor and departs before your eyes.

Other conditions can also change, sometimes so imperceptibly that you hardly notice until something in your composition starts to look wrong. The movement of the tide is a good example of this.

In *Low tide at Lynmouth* (Devon) on the left, it was important that I completed the sketch during the period of slack water.

The *Royal Yacht Britannia*, above, moored at Dartmouth, Devon, obviously wasn't going anywhere in a hurry. It was a bright day and the clouds were few and low.

It is of course not always possible to predict changes in the weather particularly in the UK. Shadows and reflections can disappear in an instant so, if you intend to make a feature of these, it is best to choose a sunny day with little cloud.

Above all, try to make sure that you're going to be as physically comfortable as possible for as long as it takes to complete your drawing.

Basic composition

Image placement

Every artist, including myself, has had the experience of trying to draw a scene by starting in the top left-hand corner and running out of paper before getting everything in.

The best way to avoid this is to decide, before you start, on the approximate extent and layout of the drawing, as well as the scale and area of paper it is going to occupy.

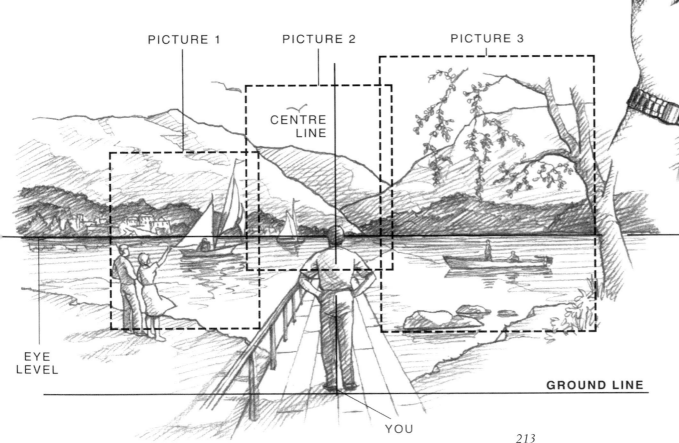

Assuming you have a field of vision such as in the illustration on the left, it is possible to decide straightaway which area will make the most interesting composition.

Having chosen an area to focus on, it will help to frame the subject. You can do this by using the thumb and forefinger of both hands to form a rudimentary rectangle in front of your face.

You can do the same thing, more accurately, by cutting out and holding up two L-shaped pieces of stiff card. This method also allows you to vary the shape and size of the rectangle, as in the illustration above.

213

Balancing the composition

In order to make quite sure I get the most from the scene in terms of composition, I like to make a series of rapid 'thumbnail' sketches.

It really is worth spending five minutes roughing in the main features of the picture. This not only clarifies the general layout and balance of the drawing, but it also helps to identify the focal points as well as the stronger areas of tone and contrast.

Hope Cove, Devon.

Kingsbridge, Devon.

Falmouth, Cornwall.

Dartmouth, Devon.

With each composition I have tried to create a careful balance between a strong feature in the foreground, an interesting middle ground and a well-defined horizon.

Scribbling in the main areas of tone, keeping them to just three gradations – light grey, mid-grey and black – helps to determine whether the composition is going to work. Too large an area of white or black in the wrong place will unbalance the picture.

214

Features and focal points

Because of the wealth of strong visual material in most harbours, it is not always easy to be selective in what you draw.

If you are a recent convert to the joys of sketching, some subjects may prove rather too complex or detailed to tackle, even if you're prepared to spend all day on one drawing – which I wouldn't recommend.

Allow yourself two hours at most for one sketch and, having worked out the framing, decide how much of the total area will be occupied by the main feature. This could be a single boat, a small group of little boats or a shore-based feature such as a lighthouse.

The angle at which you view the main feature will, to a great extent, determine what occupies the rest of the picture area.

This fishing boat was viewed from the promenade above the harbour at Newquay in Cornwall. Because any distant features, like the horizon, were excluded, the composition was uncomplicated.

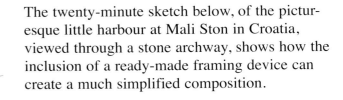

The twenty-minute sketch below, of the picturesque little harbour at Mali Ston in Croatia, viewed through a stone archway, shows how the inclusion of a ready-made framing device can create a much simplified composition.

This also obviated the need for any thought about the limits of the picture area. I only had to decide how close I would sit to the arch.

215

Decision time

What to put in and what to leave out

The framing exercises and thumbnail sketches will have helped you to decide what's important in the overall composition. It is entirely up to you to determine exactly what you include.

Just because an object appears within your frame doesn't mean you are obliged to show it in the drawing.

You should find that if you allocate about half of your time to the main feature(s) and/or foreground, then you will have to be fairly selective about how much detail you have time to put into the middle and far distance.

Both images on this page were sufficiently interesting in themselves that, working on the old design principle of less is more, I felt it unnecessary to add anything else.

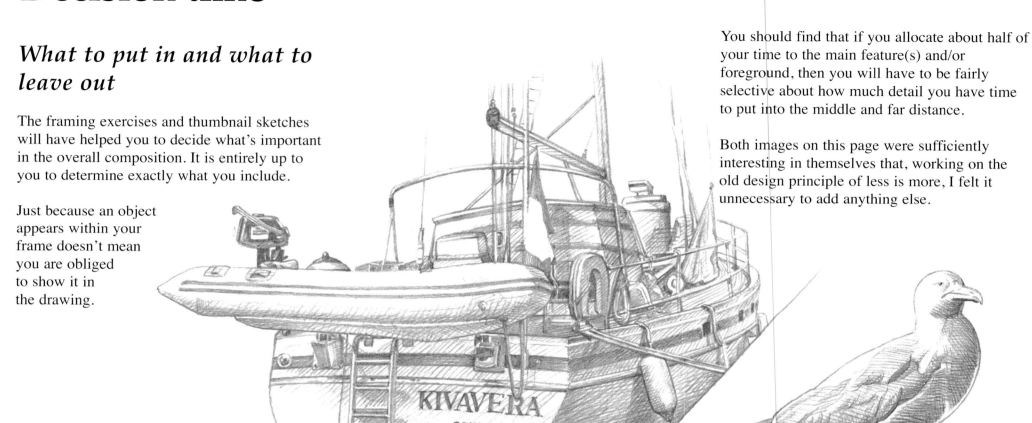

KIVAVERA

TOULON

On the other hand, you could find yourself in a situation where there is no discernible foreground feature.

This view of the commercial dock at Falmouth, Cornwall, seen from the fishing port, is to all intents and purposes a flat panorama. I have tried to place more emphasis upon the large crane on the left of the picture in order to give the composition more of a focal point.

Normally, with a subject like this, I would have ignored the sailing boats moored at the small jetty on the right but in this case I felt that the sketch desperately needed something in the middle distance to create depth.

What you see and what you know

Sketching is based primarily upon observation. However, memory and understanding also play a part in helping to decide how we represent what we see.

The more we take note of our surroundings, the better equipped we are to deal with new visual experiences.

Nonetheless, it is often the case that the way things look superficially does not tell the whole story of how they are constructed or how they actually work.

The gargoyle on the right is a good example of this. I discovered its real purpose by happy accident. I had walked past the baroque church of St Blaise in Dubrovnik, Croatia, many times without really noticing these grotesque stone heads which appeared every three meters or so at about eye level.

It was not until I was caught in a sudden, torrential rainstorm that I realised they had a purpose. They were outlets for the surface water from the roof which gushed down the side of the building through concealed conduits.

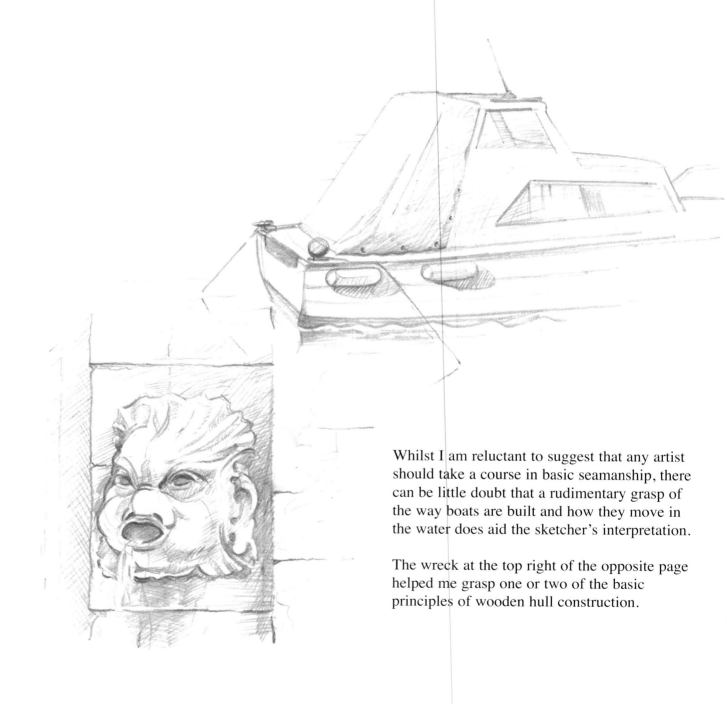

Whilst I am reluctant to suggest that any artist should take a course in basic seamanship, there can be little doubt that a rudimentary grasp of the way boats are built and how they move in the water does aid the sketcher's interpretation.

The wreck at the top right of the opposite page helped me grasp one or two of the basic principles of wooden hull construction.

Gathering reference

One of the more practical applications of sketching is to glean visual information for more detailed drawings or for developing initial ideas into fully-fledged works of art.

By analysing and noting the form of a yacht, the structure of a sea-wall or the wingbeats of a gull with a few simple lines, we create a valuable record, particularly in circumstances where there is probably only one opportunity in a lifetime to witness a particular scene of a unique event.

It is also a useful habit always to carry a camera so that you can capture the fleeting movements which can sometimes bring a picture to life.

The drawing on the left could not have been completed without resorting to photography to record the two people who suddenly appeared and began to have a conversation while I was sketching their catamaran.

Photographs can also be used to record light conditions and colours which may alter if the weather changes before you've finished the drawing.

Analysing the scene

Sightlines and horizons

Trying to find a simple relationship between foreground, middle ground and distance is not always easy.

One solution that I have found very useful in this respect is to establish a framework with a reasonable amount of sky or water occupying the top or bottom of the picture.

In many cases you will find, as in the sketch of Whitby harbour on the right, that you can employ both features to create a comfortable balance. In this case, the only feature in the foreground is the seagull.

From a high position, sitting on a hilltop or with a clear view out to sea for example, your eye level will coincide precisely with the horizon that you can see.

More often than not the limit of your sight, or 'false horizon', will be defined by rooftops or the hills behind them.

Whitby, North Yorkshire.

221

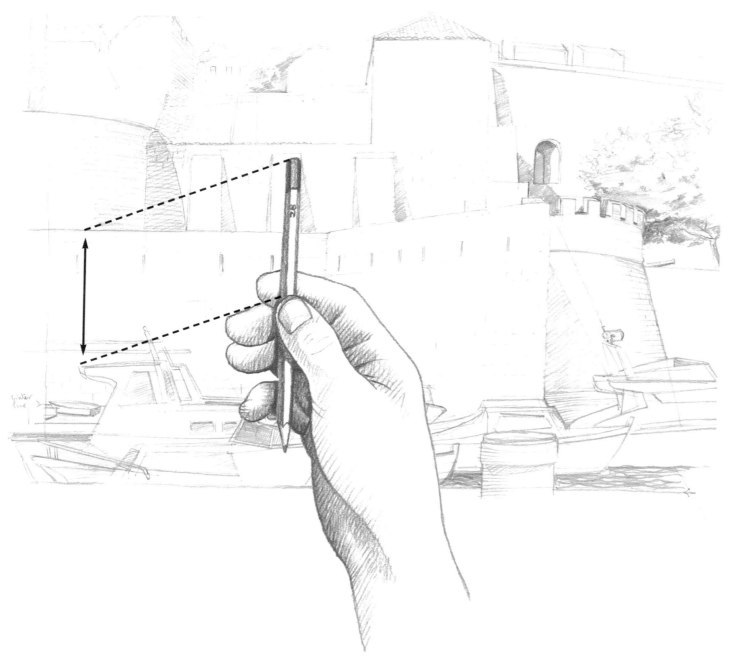

Judging size and distance

Any artist will tell you that the most significant skill you can develop is the ability to evaluate the relative scale of what you see.

Fortunately nature has endowed most of us with the capacity to judge distance fairly well at a glance. What is more difficult is to work out how big everything is according to its distance from your eye.

The tried and trusted, and quite literal, rule of thumb method of visual measurement for sketching purposes is to hold your pencil, as shown on the left, at arm's length and to place the tip of your thumb against it as if you were reading off units on a scale.

If you notice, for example, that a building in the foreground is roughly as high as the length of the pencil and a building in the middle distance is half of the pencil's length then you can transpose these ratios to your sketch.

Similarly the pencil gauge can help you to judge horizontal distances as well as angles – particularly useful when calculating the height and angle of a ship's mast and rigging.

TRUE HORIZON (eye level)

50–60 km——

400 m——

100 m——

50 m——

10 m——

5 m——

3 m——

0 ——

—— 35 m

——33 m

——30 m

——25 m

——20 m

——15 m

——10 m

——0

Here is a useful little exercise in judging size and distance. Try marking off a series of equal units down each side of your picture. Then add, in metres, the heights and distances which you think are roughly equivalent to the position of the main features in your composition.

The drawing above, for which I was looking down from a clifftop villa in Ibiza, gave me a fairly good indication of distance because I had a clear view of the horizon. The real problem, however, was to overcome the illusion which makes objects appear closer than they would be if everything were laid out in front of you on the same flat plane, like men on a chessboard.

Looking at the sketch on the right you can see how much more difficult it is to judge distances. At the same time, because everything is based just above or just below eye level, it is a lot easier to work out relative heights.

Lynmouth, Devon.

Simple perspective

There is no great scientific mystery about working out the perspective of any vista provided you follow a few easy rules.

For the purpose of this book we will stick to the two basic methods – single and two point perspective.

Single point

On the right is a drawing based upon one vanishing point only. The vanishing point will always appear on your eye level which, in this case, represents the centre of your vision and coincides precisely with the visible true horizon.

Having established the position of the vanishing point it may help to sketch in lightly a number of diagonal lines along which to locate all the vital features of your composition.

Two point

The diagram on the opposite page is similar but, instead of one, there are two vanishing points beyond the left and right limits of the area of vision. These are located, once again, on your eye level but instead of using the centre line to calculate where they meet the eye level, you'll need to find clues within your area of vision.

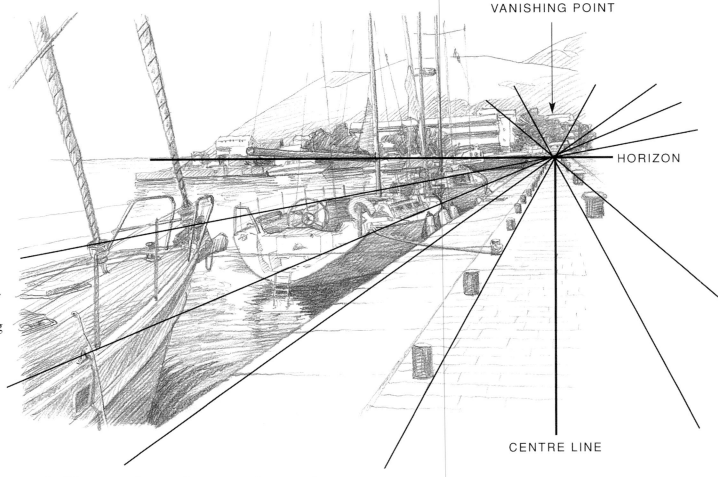

VANISHING POINT

HORIZON

CENTRE LINE

In this scene, the two important clues are the angle of the quayside in the bottom left corner and the waterline at the base of the further harbour wall which, in reality, is situated at right angles to the nearer quayside. These are the 'key angles'.

Having established the two vanishing points, the good news is that by projecting any diagonal from one or both, all your ground lines (e.g. for helping to gauge the relative heights of figures at different distances), as well as the roofline angles should be spot on.

There are, of course, more complex ways of calculating the more difficult issues of pictorial perspective but, if you concentrate to start with on the two more basic ones as illustrated here, you shouldn't go far wrong.

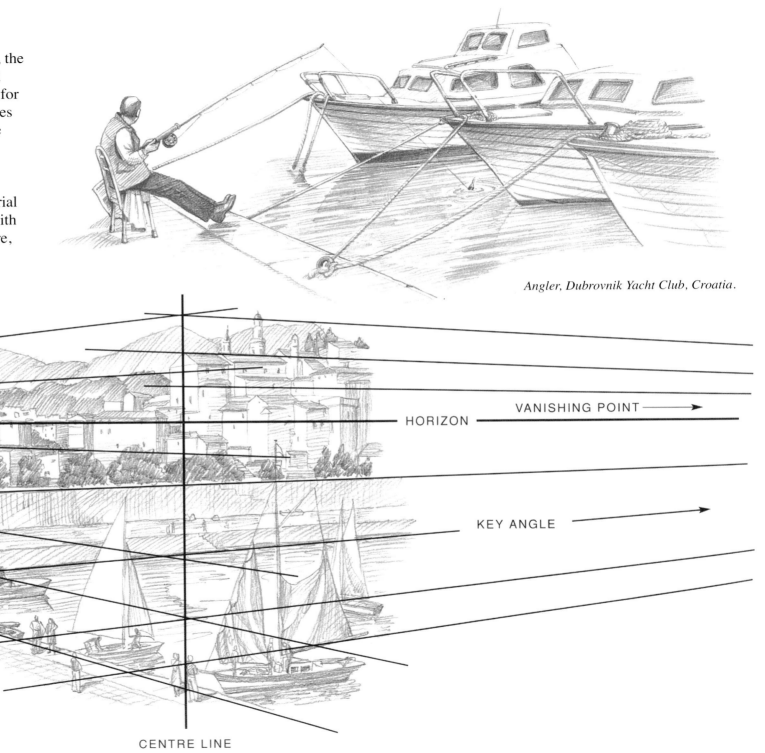

Angler, Dubrovnik Yacht Club, Croatia.

VANISHING POINT

VANISHING POINT

HORIZON

KEY ANGLE

KEY ANGLE

CENTRE LINE

Understanding light

Creating form

At the risk of stating the obvious, the reason we find it difficult to see anything properly in the dark is simply that, without light, form does not exist as a visual entity.

Conversely when we try to copy the formal aspects of an object onto paper it is that effect of light which ultimately creates the most convincing impression.

In order to incorporate a recognition of how the light is affecting the subject in your drawing it helps to work out first where it is coming from.

The easiest way to understand the idea of this is to think about how only one side of the earth has daylight at any one time – when it is light in the northern hemisphere it is dark in the southern hemisphere because it is on the opposite side of the earth and facing away from the light source, the sun.

Similarly, a drawing of any basic form will begin to appear visually more three dimensional if, having determined the direction of the main source of light, we add the tonal effects that represent light and shade.

It is well worth practising this exercise using only the most basic of geometric models before attempting to apply this theory to more complicated shapes. Start with a standard cube or box shape.

ANGLE OF SHADOW

DIRECTION OF LIGHT

ANGLE OF SHADOW

DIRECTION OF LIGHT

Now try reproducing the effects of direct light on a series of spheres and cones in different positions relative to light sources of differing strengths and directions.

When you feel confident enough you could try tackling more complicated forms.

Even though it constituted only a small part of the intended picture, this ornate, nineteenth-century, iron lamp-post on the quayside at Dubrovnik, Croatia, kept me occupied for nearly an hour.

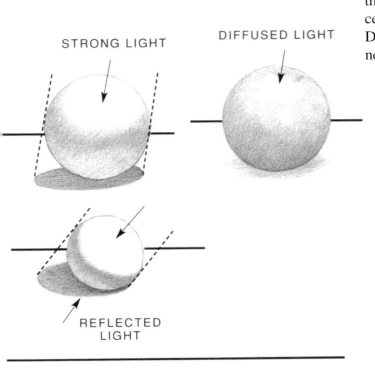

STRONG LIGHT

DIFFUSED LIGHT

REFLECTED LIGHT

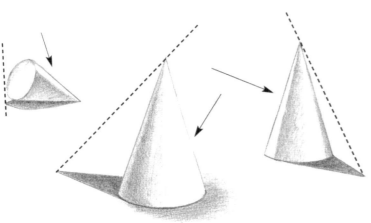

Definition

Although enhancing the appearance of form will help considerably in conveying the impression of reality, it is also desirable if you can find ways of differentiating clearly where one shape ends and the adjacent area begins.

The way we see things naturally is really the greatest ally in this process but occasionally nature needs a little artistic licence in the interpretation.

A good, strong line around the focus of your composition will help it to stand out against the background, as will a generous helping of white space around an object.

Salcombe, Devon.

There really is no substitute for making a few quick thumbnail sketches to determine how dark and light areas are going to work together and where lines or shadows need strengthening to make an item stand out from its surroundings.

Generally speaking, the brighter the light you are working in, the easier it is to create dramatic contrasts within your picture.

Dubrovnik, Croatia.

Falmouth, Cornwall.

Contrasts are always more marked when things are close to our eye. In order to give sketches more depth and sense of space an artist will often overemphasize the lack of detail and definition in distant features.

In this sketch of two boys sitting on railings at Dartmouth in Devon I have tried to convey a sense of distance by accentuating the contrasting tones in the railings as well as drawing a dark outline with a soft pencil around the figures themselves.

Conversely, for the houses and trees on the other side of the river, I've used a harder pencil to reduce the amount of contrast and give a more monotonal impression.

Shadows and reflections

Of all the problems involved in drawing, this is the area which seems to cause the most puzzlement and frustration.

The earlier section on creating form should help a little with the angles of shadows. Working out the direction from which light is hitting the subject is always half the battle.

Beyond this, a good general rule is: the brighter a single light source is in relation to its surroundings the sharper will be the edge of the actual shadow of the objects.

Unless the favour sketching at night, then the chances are that the biggest determining factor will be the strength and position of the sun. At dawn and dusk the shadows cast by objects will always be much longer than at noon when the sun is directly overhead.

The ambient softness of outdoor light in northern Europe means that a few of the sketches in this book can easily illustrate the above points.

I was lucky enough, however, to be able to sketch this boy repairing his fibreglass dinghy at Salcombe, Devon, on a particularly sunny day.

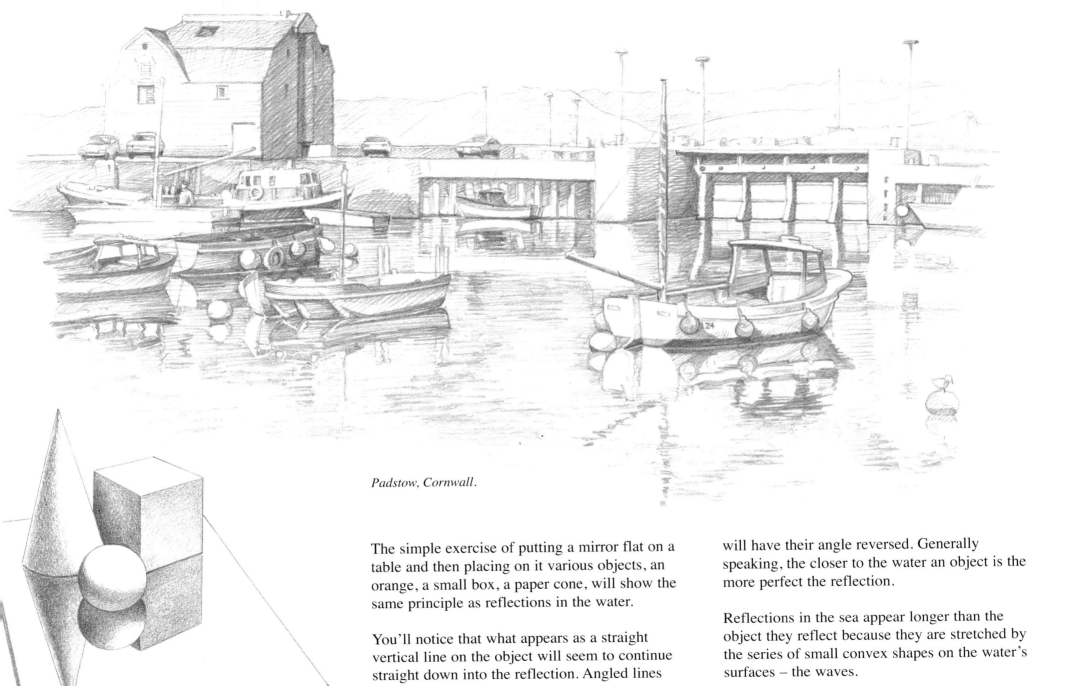

Padstow, Cornwall.

The simple exercise of putting a mirror flat on a table and then placing on it various objects, an orange, a small box, a paper cone, will show the same principle as reflections in the water.

You'll notice that what appears as a straight vertical line on the object will seem to continue straight down into the reflection. Angled lines will have their angle reversed. Generally speaking, the closer to the water an object is the more perfect the reflection.

Reflections in the sea appear longer than the object they reflect because they are stretched by the series of small convex shapes on the water's surfaces – the waves.

231

Bringing drawings to life

Adding figures

The simplest way to create interest in a
composition is to include some animate
feature – human activity is the most obvious
example, but birds, dogs, cats and horses will
do almost as well.

The big problem, of course, is that, except in
rare cases, people are not going to maintain the
same position for the amount of time that it
takes to do any more than rough in their
outline and main features.

If a detailed and accurate drawing is your ultimate aim, then the camera will capture the detail to be added late whilst leaving you free to concentrate on the rest of the image.

Whenever I get the chance I like to draw the more unusual activities of people and animals. Those involved with boats and water tend to present a good number of such opportunities. My favourite moment over the past year of sketching was when I was lucky enough to spot this gull catching a large eel.

Getting the scale of figures exactly right within their surroundings is often the cause of artists' problems. Everyone, including me, tends to make people too big. Believe me, nothing looks less convincing than a ten-foot man standing in a six-foot boat.

Whether they're distant specks crewing a racing yacht or incidental bystanders on a jetty, it is essential to measure visually the height of figures by comparing them with any nearby feature, such as a ship's mast.

Conveying movement

One could regard investing a drawing with a sense of movement as something of a challenge. It is not always easy to follow a sequence of activity with the naked eye and capture the essence of it on paper.

Nonetheless, the combination of boats and water does create such opportunities, particularly when billowing sails or a white-capped bow wave is in evidence.

Stormy seas can also offer the opportunity to convey a more dramatic kind of movement. This sketch on the right, of the outer harbour wall at Lynmouth, Devon, was begun on the beach but had to be completed in the studio because of the atrocious weather.

The young man posing in the rubber dinghy on the facing page was obviously keen to create an image and was travelling at considerable speed. Neither my sketchbook nor a photograph could adequately impart this. In the drawing which was done later in the studio, I was able to overemphasize the tilt of the boat and the wake of white water behind the outboard motor.

Yacht race at Porto Cervo, Sardinia.

The old sailing barge on the left is a complete contrast. As it was cruising along at a leisurely pace, the detail of the bow wave is really the only clue that it is moving at all.

The gull on the right was disappearing so fast when I saw it that I had to sketch the shape of its wings very rapidly and add the detail of its feathers and so on by guesswork.

If you are a beginner, it is probably best if you avoid rapidly moving objects until you have really gained some confidence in your technique.

Mood and atmosphere

Conventionally it is drawings of a lower key or darker overall tone value which are imbued with a good deal more sentiment than those in a high key, or relatively light overall tone – such as the lad in the dinghy on page 235.

The drawing on the right shows the port of Anacona in Italy at dawn. I have deliberately tried to reduce the contrast and soften the edges of the ships and cranes in the foreground by using a 6B pencil with a well-rounded point – if that's not a contradiction in terms.

An added sense of drama in this sketch is created by the image of the sun bursting into an overcast sky from behind the city. The detail of the city itself was scarcely visible with the skyline forming a strong silhouette.

The use of a very soft pencil on watercolour paper creates a grainy appearance and reduces the differentiation between areas of tone even further.

The sketch below is of Barmouth in Wales at low tide, at dusk on a warm summer evening.

To create mood, the key is again kept deliberately low, although smoother paper and a harder pencil have been used to render the boats on the sandbar in sharper relief. This artificial level of foreground contrast helps to make the bridge in the middle ground, and the hills in the background, recede.

Alternative media

Even though this book is really all about sketching with pencils, there is a variety of other sketching implements which can be used to create many different effects. There are two main groups: pens and brushes: charcoals and pastels.

Pens and brushes

A lot of people use fibretips, biros or even fountain pens for jotting down quick impressions in a sketchbook.

Thin, fibretipped pen sketch of Whitby harbour, North Yorkshire.

Whilst you do lose some of the subtle tonal qualities of a pencil drawing, ink or watercolour pens are convenient, clean and the results do not need spraying with fixative.

Rendering the line work in waterproof ink gives you the option of applying water-based wash on top of the original sketch. This technique is called 'line and wash'.

The drawing at the top of Whitby quayside at dusk was done in situ with a black ink Flo-pen. The wash was added later using a brush and a thin solution of black gouache.

Having observed and interpreted the outlines and basic structure of the subject in pencil, one of the most popular media for adding tonal variation is watercolour.

This can be applied in situ if you have sufficient time or later using notes and/or photographic reference.

The outline sketch should, if possible, be rendered on paper which won't stretch or cockle when the paint is applied – for instance, Not or semi-rough watercolour paper.

One of the more recent inventions that has served to make the itinerant artist's life considerably easier and less messy is water-soluble pencils.

The painting on the left was originally drawn on Watman paper using Aquarelle water-soluble pencils and the tonal wash added at the same time by 'painting' with water only. The subject is an ancient, stone archway at Mali Ston in Croatia which was in the process of being renovated, having been damaged in 1997 by an earthquake.

Charcoal and pastels

Whilst being a fairly crude medium by comparison with pencils, charcoal has a strength and vibrancy which make it ideal for creating dramatic contrasts.

Soft charcoal pencil on CS2 paper – Hope cove, Devon.

For those who don't mind getting dirty fingers and who have sufficient delicacy to avoid transferring black smudges onto the drawing surface, traditional charcoal sticks are great fun to use.

These days, however, there is a variety of charcoal pensils not dissimilar from ordinary pencils. Nevertheless, I would always advise making a light pencil sketch before launching into a full-blooded charcoal drawing.

Both oil pastels and pastel crayons give something of the flavour of working directly with paints but without the bother of having to clean brushes or wait for colours to dry.

It may be advisable, however, to equip yourself with a box of tissues and some thinners in a small jar, just to clean up dirty fingers and avoid smudges as you go along.

Again I would suggest doing an outline pencil sketch before applying either of these dense media. Oil pastels in particular are pretty unforgiving so try to work from light to dark, saving areas of deep shadow until the end.

The sketch on the left, a yacht race at Salcombe, Devon, was produced with a black graphite pencil on CS2 paper. I would equally well have used pastel sticks to create a similar effect.

Above, the little fishing harbour at Mali Ston, Croatia, was 'painted' with pastel sticks, an instant medium, which, if you're careful, can be worked over – especially if you fix the underneath layer first.

241

Finishing touches

Highlights and definition

In order to add that extra sparkle to your work it is sometimes a good idea to strengthen the outlines of foreground features, deepen shadows or add whiter highlights to the final result.

If you're working in graphite pencils it is quite straightforward to go ove the dark areas with a softer, or blacker, pencil. Highlights can then be added either with a hard rubber sharpened to a point or a fine paintbrush and Process White, a virtually opaque, water-based medium similar to gouache.

Pastels, as mentioned on the previous page, can be 'overpainted'. Oil pastels are easier to alter as the colour is more opaque. This drawing, of the Old City port at Dubrovnik, Croatia, was drawn in chalky pastels on grey Canson paper.

Then it was complete, I fixed it, mainly to protect the dusty surface, and then, when it was dry, I revived the shadows and highlights with pure black and pure white pastel sticks.

Protecting your work

Charcoal, pastel and even pencil drawings do not take kindly to being handled roughly. If you can, always use a light coating of clear spray fixative or, if you're really stuck, try hair lacquer – which is a cheaper altenative.

Unfortunately, any protective spray has the disadvantage of darkening the image.

If you think there is a danger that your skilfully-crafted pencil gradations of tone might lose some of their subtlety, simply cover the work with a sheet of thin tissue paper and avoid touching the surface.

Sketchbook page – details of a car ferry, Split, Croatia.

Mounting and framing

I hope you will be proud enough of your efforts at sketching harbours and boats to want to display your work for all to see.

Monochromatic drawings are best shown in simple frames. I tend to go for plain, thin, grey beading or just steel clips and glass.

If you feel a mount is necessary, other than a plain white surround, choose muted or pastel colours as they tend to complement grey and black images rather better than bright reds, blues and greens.

I wish you well in your endeavours and I sincerely hope that you will enjoy, as I have, the unique pleasures that come from filling a sketchbook with your experiences.

Transporter bridge,
Newcastle-upon-Tyne,
Northumbria.

Part 5
Sketching Street Scenes

Sketching in towns

Here are a few of the special difficulties likely to be encountered at the outset, together with some suggestions to help overcome them.

A basic understanding of perspective is a key requirement when drawing buildings and structures. Also, the appropriate inclusion of people or human interest is highly desirable if the street scenes are not to look like the aftermath of some dreadful catastrophe. Both of these factors are dealt with in as much detail as space allows in later stages of this book.

On a more general level, it is much harder to work unobserved in towns than in the wide open spaces. Unless you possess outstanding self confidence or have an aspiration to become a performance artist, it is advisable not to set up an easel on a street corner; there are a number of alternatives which are fairly effective. Get your back up against something so that an audience can't form behind you. (I thought I had achieved this once by sitting against a sea wall only to hear a comment from a small crowd above me.) On the other hand, standing propped against a wall glancing up frequently and making marks in a small notebook can make one look suspiciously like a private detective or a villain planning a robbery.

Once a group of council gardeners began working frantically as I drew them, in the mistaken belief that I was an official conducting a time and motion study. After I told them this was not the case they relaxed into more suitably recumbent poses.

It is much more comfortable and less conspicuous if you are able to sit down to make a sketch. Park benches are good except you can become a sitting target for every passer-by with time on their hands and problems to share; overhead pigeons may also want to join in the fun. A small inflatable cushion can make sitting on walls and steps a more attractive option.

The ultimate luxury is to draw from a cafe or a bar accompanied by an amiable companion and an appropriate beverage. Some of my most enjoyable memories are associated with this gentle activity, either outdoors in warm weather or captured through windows whilst sheltering from the elements.

If you avoid peak periods and look out for traffic wardens, a car can provide good vantage points, privacy and shelter and, in the case of my camper van, occasional refreshments.

Gathering information

A commission from my local town council to produce a series of line drawings featuring places of local interest started me drawing street scenes. Without this challenge I would probably have stuck to country landscapes, but once I got started I found it very absorbing.

Unfortunately, when I know my work is going to be printed, I find it is harder to maintain the freedom and spontaneity which comes with drawing purely for pleasure. Drawing within imposed time limits means that I sometimes can't help producing some rather 'tight' drawings, such as the one on the right, an example of this rather more laborious and detailed approach.

Sketchbooks can be used for collecting visual information which may later be put together in more finished compositions. For example, studies of people, animals or small details. A camera is also handy if you run short of time.

Drawing directly with a pen without any preliminary pencil work forces you to sum up a situation in the simplest terms. If a line is wrong you have to 'overdraw' the first mark because it is impossible to rub out. This is a good way of developing your personal 'visual handwriting'.

Using a pen which you don't have to keep dipping into an ink bottle can assist in the speed of a drawing. For this reason, some artists use a fibre-tipped, a fountain or a ballpoint pen.

Tuesday 26th August
Afternoon mint tea
outside the Café de Paris
'watching the world
go by'

Traffic police
in the place de
France

Basic equipment

Sketching outdoors requires one to travel light, carrying only a small selection of tried and trusted tools and equipment which will fit into a pocket or a small bag. Use of simple and familiar tools, such as pencils or pens, is less conspicuous if working outdoors on location. To some extent your choice of these will influence your approach, direct what you look at and the information you are able to put down.

Pencils

For fine details, it is better to use well sharpened H grade pencils and smooth paper surfaces. For broad tonal impressions, try soft B grade pencils, charcoal, crayons or pastels and rough-surfaced papers.

You will need to keep sharpening soft pencils, so have a craft knife or sharpener with you. Kneadable erasers can be shaped to a point, enabling you to rub out, lighten or highlight specific areas. Use your fingers or specially made, rolled cardboard torchons to blend tones, and remember to spray your work with fixative so it doesn't smudge.

Water-soluble pencils combine the advantages of normal graphite with the capability of creating washes when wet. For this I carry water in a 35mm film cassette case and a small watercolour paintbrush.

HB graphite pencil on smooth cartridge paper.

Soft and hard graphite pencils combined.

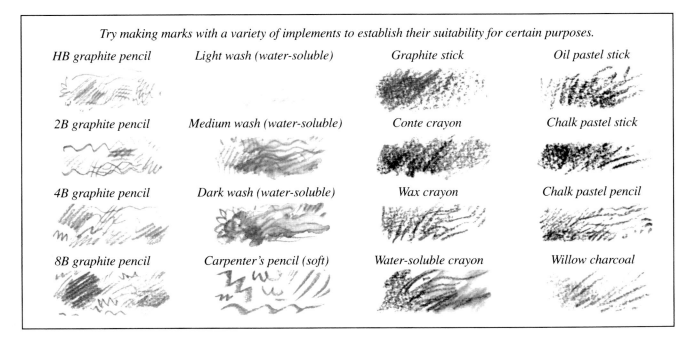

Try making marks with a variety of implements to establish their suitability for certain purposes.

HB graphite pencil	Light wash (water-soluble)	Graphite stick	Oil pastel stick
2B graphite pencil	Medium wash (water-soluble)	Conte crayon	Chalk pastel stick
4B graphite pencil	Dark wash (water-soluble)	Wax crayon	Chalk pastel pencil
8B graphite pencil	Carpenter's pencil (soft)	Water-soluble crayon	Willow charcoal

Pens and brushes

There should be no problem finding a pen and brush of your choice since there is a plethora of them in the shops. While they are cheap and portable, both of which are very handy, watch out for the occasional disadvantage – some fibre-tips will run if you put a wash over them; others have a tendency to bleed through one or more sheets of paper.

It is important to be able to create a contrast in line thickness if you want your drawings to have vitality, so consider using a range of instruments – rollerballs, brush pens, fine liners, technical and calligraphy pens.

'Dip' pens give a variety of marks. Use them with inks which are either 'fixed' or waterproof when dry, or 'unfixed' which are not. They have the advantage over other pens and brushes because they do not clog up.

You can cut, sharpen and customize reed pens, bamboo pens and quills.

Steel nibs, fitted into holders, come in various widths and their mark on paper is dictated by how hard you press.

To avoid fountain sketching pens clogging up, use them with unfixed ink.

Sable and synthetic hair brushes can be bought in many forms and sizes. A 'rigger', a brush with long hair used by nautical painters to draw in the fine lines of rigging, can be almost like a pencil to draw with.

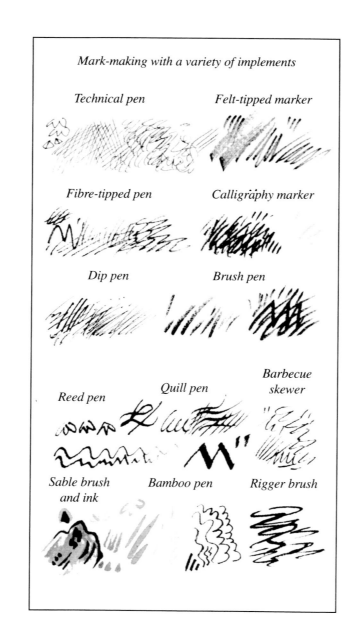

Mark-making with a variety of implements

Technical pen   Felt-tipped marker

Fibre-tipped pen   Calligraphy marker

Dip pen   Brush pen

Reed pen   Quill pen   Barbecue skewer

Sable brush and ink   Bamboo pen   Rigger brush

Pen sketch on smooth paper. Tones have to be made by crosshatched lines.

Line and wash sketch on watercolour paper. Begun with a water-resistant, fibre-tipped pen, the tonal ink washes were applied afterwards with a sable brush.

Types of paper

The choice of sketchbook should be influenced by its function. Size and weight are big factors to consider if you intend to carry it with you every day. Sturdy binding will be a big advantage if it is going to have to travel well. At the expensive end of the market are handmade and bound watercolour books; beautiful but perhaps a touch daunting. More practical are the low-cost cartridge pads. Even cheaper still are individual sheets of paper and a drawing board or clipboard.

Paper

In general there are three types of surface:
- smooth or 'hot pressed' (mechanically pressed through hot rollers) which is suitable for fine detail and pen work;
- semi-rough or 'not' pressed which will suit most purposes;
- rough and textured papers which suit broader treatments.

Paper has different thicknesses, or 'weights', and absorbencies, which make it either more or less suitable for wash treatments. Generally speaking, a watercolour sketchbook and heavier weight papers will cover most options. Cheaper lightweight papers must be 'stretched' on a drawing board so that they do not buckle when water is applied to them.

Pen sketch on smooth, 'hot pressed' paper. Ideal for quick line drawing in pen or harder grade pencils.

Brush drawing on semi-rough watercolour paper without preliminary pencil work.

Pencil on inexpensive cartridge paper. The smooth surface is ideal for general drawing and detailed work.

Pen line and wash sketch on watercolour paper. A pen draws the linework first; loose washes are then applied.

Locations and subjects

Everyday locations can become more interesting as you begin to draw them and it is not really necessary to go far in search of subject matter.

Somehow qualities seem to emerge as we get into looking closely and trying to represent honestly what we see. Time spent in looking before drawing is seldom wasted but it is important not to become paralysed with fear at the enormity of the task ahead of you.

Drawing shouldn't be a tedious activity; if you get bored just simplify or leave out things you don't find interesting. On the other hand, bring in other things you want to include or move them about to add to your composition.

The landscape is in a constant state of change, especially in towns, where your drawings can become unique historical records of buildings or local characteristics which may be eliminated or modified by redevelopment schemes.

Make a list of some possible areas of interest which might yield promising subject matter or may in turn become themes for a whole series of drawings. Here are a few examples – pubs, street markets, car boot sales, back gardens, allotments, parks and sportsfields, cinemas, street entertainers, railway stations or sidings, bridges, cemeteries and monuments.

I SAW IT FIRST!

Basic shapes and components

Complex forms found in architecture can be confusing to draw so a suggestion is to see if they could be based on more simplified geometric shapes, rather like children's toy bricks. Try basing them on a framework of cubes, rectangles, cones or cylinders before adding any elaboration and surface details; this gives a better understanding of the way that light can fall on structures and make them look more three-dimensional. This approach can also be applied to other objects within the landscape such a motor cars, telephone kiosks and even trees.

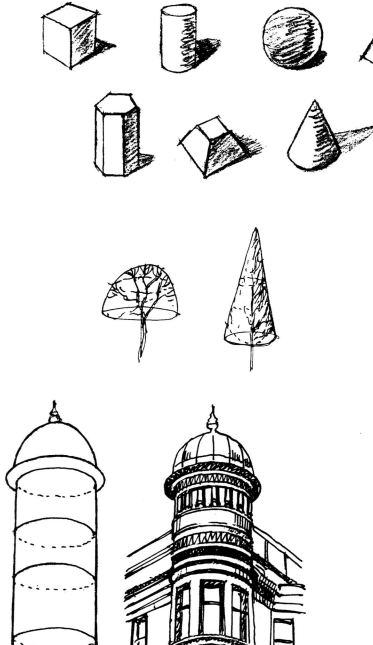

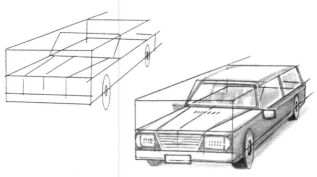

Perspective

Try not to be daunted as you start drawing by the knowledge that your sense of perspective could be better. It is something that will improve vastly if you follow these guidelines and you will soon find that you are able to make convincing visual representations of objects in space.

To create an illusion of depth and recession, there must be a contrast between foreground, middle ground and distance. A sketch can contain visual clues to give the viewer an idea of distance.

Items in the foreground are larger and more distinct; the further away they are, the fainter and less defined they become.

This is called 'atmospheric perspective'. Emphasize this difference with a distinct tonal contrast in foreground and background layers.

There are various other clues – overlapping areas, forms and contours, which define whether one thing is in front of another, and the intervals between similar sized elements such as windows, streetlamps or paving stones appearing to diminish in size as they recede in the distance.

ATMOSPHERIC PERSPECTIVE

The horizon is easy to see when we look out to sea – it is the line between the sea and the sky. However, it is less obvious with a landscape.

The position on the page of the horizon line creates a subdivision between the areas of land and sky. Dynamic compositions can be achieved by allowing one or the other to dominate, rather than making everything symmetrical.

The horizon can be raised or lowered on the page to reflect the focus of your interests. To attract the eye to the sky, make the horizon lower down on the page.

The same can be said if you want to look down on a scene.

To concentrate more on the foreground, have a higher horizon.

To keep everything in the sketch in perspective, all structures or elements in the landscape have to be drawn in relation to the established horizon.

ONE POINT PERSPECTIVE

HORIZON

VP

The general rule is that all receding parallel lines above your eye level appear to slant down towards the horizon while those below eye level travel upward. The point on which these converge is called the vanishing point (VP).

'One point perspective', as illustrated above, describes the situation observed when there may be only one obvious vanishing point.

An exercise that will help you with perspective is to lay tracing paper over a photograph of some buildings and, with a ruler, trace lines which seem to converge so that you can see where they intersect. This will indicate the camera level and the point at which the lens was focused when the photograph was taken.

TWO POINT PERSPECTIVE

VP 1

VP 2

When looking at a building corner-on, with its sides receding away acutely on either side, there are two vanishing points, one to the left and the other to the right, as illustrated above. This is commonly known as **'two point perspective'**.

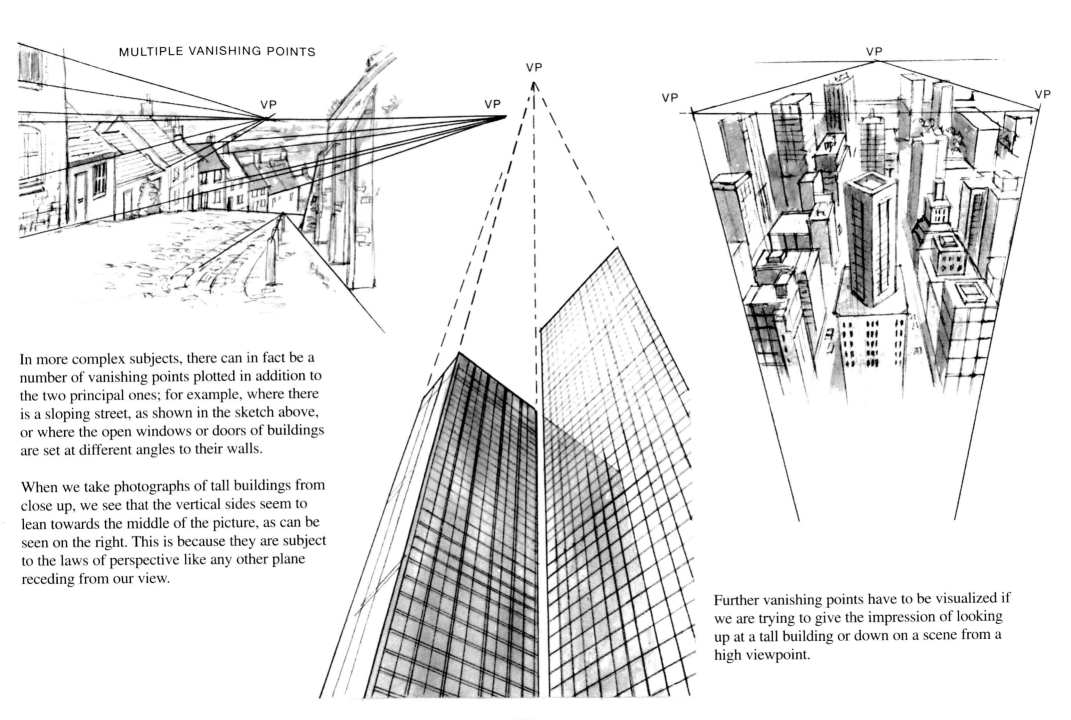

VP

VP

VP

VP

VP

VP

In more complex subjects, there can in fact be a number of vanishing points plotted in addition to the two principal ones; for example, where there is a sloping street, as shown in the sketch above, or where the open windows or doors of buildings are set at different angles to their walls.

When we take photographs of tall buildings from close up, we see that the vertical sides seem to lean towards the middle of the picture, as can be seen on the right. This is because they are subject to the laws of perspective like any other plane receding from our view.

Further vanishing points have to be visualized if we are trying to give the impression of looking up at a tall building or down on a scene from a high viewpoint.

Curves and ellipses

Fortunately the rules of perspective apply just as much to curves as to straight lines. If you are trying to draw arches, for example, there is a simple trick to assist in getting them right by fitting them first into rectangles, which can be drawn in perspective, and then establishing their centres by crossing diagonals as shown in the following diagrams.

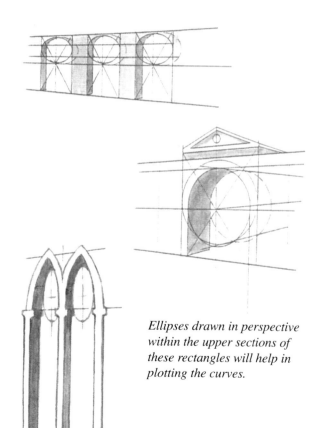

Ellipses drawn in perspective within the upper sections of these rectangles will help in plotting the curves.

The same device can be used for ellipses which can be fitted within squares drawn in perspective as shown.

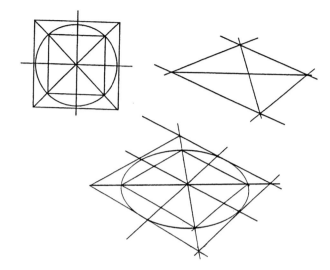

Diagram for plotting diminishing vertical intervals in perspective.

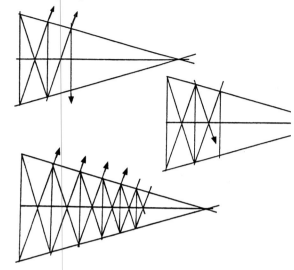

Diagram for finding the intervals between receding paving stones, in one point perspective.

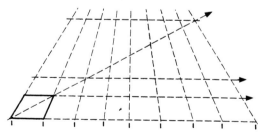

Draw the first stone in correct proportion and draw equally spaced lines to converge at the vanishing point. Project a diagonal as shown.

VP

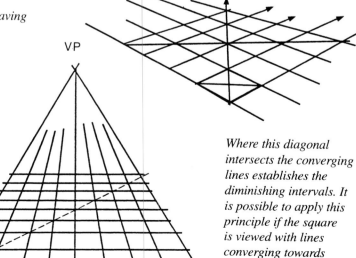

Where this diagonal intersects the converging lines establishes the diminishing intervals. It is possible to apply this principle if the square is viewed with lines converging towards two vanishing points.

Tone, light and shade

The term 'form' describes the visual appearance and shape of something. Lines and 'tones' (a range of values from light to dark) are used to represent form on paper; the addition of more tones gives an impression of greater solidity. In the sketch of the bridge, below, look first at the simple line framework and then below that at the 'modelling' effect of strong sunlight throwing areas into shadow.

The techniques of 'modelling' using tones will vary according to the media used – soft tools such as pastel, charcoal, crayon or graphite will allow you to produce large areas of tonal shading. The top illustration was done with pen and diluted ink washes. Hard pen, however, as in the drawing of the bridge at the bottom of the page, means you can render tones by crosshatched lines or stippling.

Forms and textures are revealed to us by light, but this changes throughout the day and depends upon weather conditions. We often have to be very quick to capture the effect on paper.

Strong sunlight can give hard-edged shapes, while more diffused lighting will be soft and atmospheric. It is worth concentrating on the contrasts between light and dark; remember to indicate the big shapes first before getting involved in any detail.

Sunlight and shadows

It is important to establish the location of light sources in relationship to your drawing in order to understand how or where shadows are cast. This is helpful especially in strong sunlight where they will be very pronounced. Perspective also comes into play, as shown here in these diagrams.

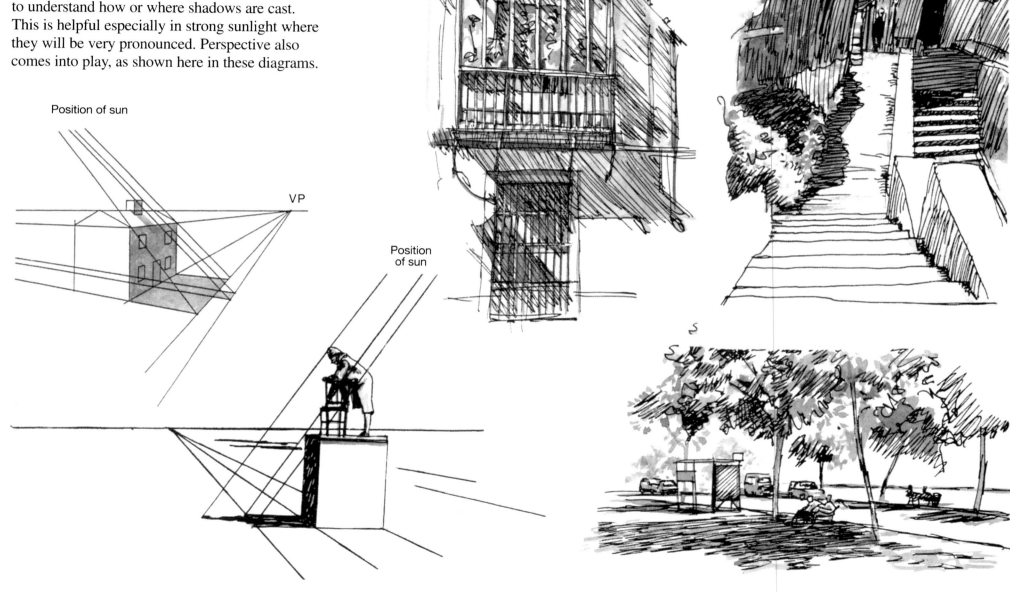

Position of sun

VP

Position of sun

Buildings and architecture

A knowledge of architecture is not necessary for sketching buildings but it will increase your enjoyment and understanding to find out something of the historic developments as you progress, and how the regional character of towns is frequently the result of the use of traditional local materials and architectural styles.

Modernization of buildings in towns and villages has often destroyed this regional charm and regrettably the concrete-box style seems to have spread almost unchecked. Of course not every redevelopment is negative and some have been notably interesting and sensitive.

In towns all the elements that go to create the environment – buildings, trees, water, advertisements, traffic and so on – are collectively woven together to produce a dramatic impact.

Some locations are more obviously inspirational than others and may have attracted painters and draughtsmen in the past. However, the challenge is to find your own situations and approaches. For instance you may be more interested in atmosphere – the play of light on buildings rather than the recording of architectural details.

Market towns as depicted in the watercolour sketch on the right are frequently rich in architectural styles.

Studies of such common objects as front doors, above, can reveal surprising variations.

In contrast to more conventionally picturesque rural landscapes, street scenes can make dramatic and fascinating subjects teeming with interest.

It's a good idea to draw in the basic immovable components before adding figures and vehicles which come and go. The building site in the sketch below right was later to become a local shopping centre and an example of recording 'history in the making'.

Old buildings offer rich areas of exploration. There are usually opportunities to discover textures and small details which might be less obvious but more interesting to draw. Attempting to render surfaces with different media is quite rewarding.

Landmarks and street furniture

Monuments, lamp-posts, pillarboxes, street signs, telephone boxes, benches, railings, bollards and a host of little unique details bring vitality, humanity and interest to our towns. They can become features worth studying in their own right or be included in pictorial compositions.

On the other hand, it sometimes assists a drawing to leave out clusters of traffic lights and signage when they would become an intrusion. We can have more control over the image in a drawing than would be possible with a photograph,

A mixture of the old and new can frequently be found in certain districts. For example, the water gate in a London park, illustrated on the right, is well over 300 years old.

Shopfronts and signage

Shopfronts and facades, some elegant and stately, some garish and tawdry, are everchanging aspects of the urban scene. Wide variation of materials – polished marble walls, plastics, sleek chrome-plated doors or lettering, the fragmented reflections of buildings twisted and distorted across windows – all become highly challenging abstract images to be drawn or photographed. Three-dimensional signs add to this rich vocabulary, as do whole buildings which are painted with eye-catching effects.

Advertising hoardings, posters, murals, graffiti, all form part of our everyday environment. Sometimes their messages or visual juxta-positions make poetic statements about present day society or lifestyles. They can help to convey a real sense of time and place. Neon at night, reflections on wet pavements, the rich patterns and collage-like accumulations of flyposters can all make exciting subject material for the artist.

Bookshop · Seville

New York Diner

Thursday 23rd August. Santa Eulalia

Transport

Some countries have retained traditional methods of transport and these in turn can be included in sketches to add further interest or authenticity. For example, bicycles are as popular as ever in Amsterdam as are the well-used trams.

I am starting to put in buses, cars, motorbikes and the like in the certain knowledge that in a few years time they will start to look very old fashioned and give my drawings a real period feel.

BRUMM BRRUMM

BAR RESTAURANTE

People watching

Nothing is quite as fascinating as watching people but it is far from easy to capture character in a quick sketch. Like a voyeur, I always try to draw without being observed, in case my subjects ask to see my efforts and complain that I haven't done them justice or I have made them look like an unflattering caricature. It's not like taking a snapshot, but speed is of the essence.

Sitting down in a corner with a small book that could pass for a private diary or a postcard, and rationing the number of times you look up at your subject is the best strategy. You have to train your visual memory and retain an after-image in your mind's eye once you look away. Of course they may move. If you are lucky they might resume the same pose but sometimes you're left with just a few precious marks and you have to fill in between, rather like a dot-to dot puzzle.

This process can be quite exhausting. All I can say is that you get better by doing it and that drawing with tools which assist in making speedy marks is essential. Maybe a pencil to begin with - since you can always draw over the top in ink if you want to. Using a pen directly without any preliminary pencilwork, as in the sketches on the right, will force you into a more precise mode, since erasure is difficult. The search for an edge or a line will result in a quality of movement rather like a multiple exposure, and I feel this can add vitality to a drawing.

Fashions, clothing and accessories

The inhabitants of modern towns are subject to constantly changing fashions in clothing and accessories. You only have to look at films taken a few years ago to observe how rapidly but almost imperceptibly these changes take place. It is worth recording them in your sketchbooks and noting how much clothing can help to define character, interests and occupations. Even without details we can define general body shapes and gestures in simple silhouette forms.

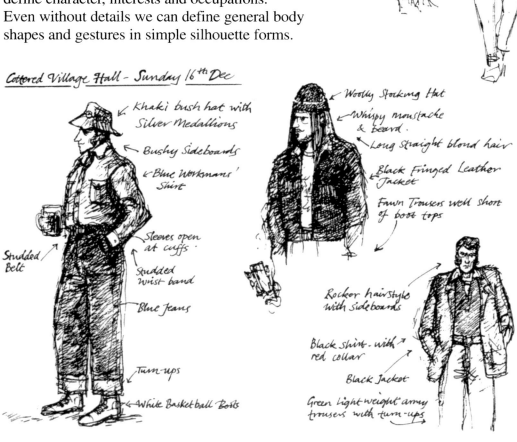

Cottered Village Hall - Sunday 16th Dec

- Khaki bush hat with Silver Medallions
- Bushy Sideboards
- Blue Workmans' Shirt
- Sleeves open at cuffs
- Studded wrist band
- Studded Belt
- Blue Jeans
- Turn-ups
- White Basketball Boots

- Woolly Stocking Hat
- Whispy moustache & beard.
- Long straight blond hair
- Black Fringed Leather Jacket
- Fawn Trousers well short of boot tops

- Rocker hairstyle with sideboards
- Black shirt with red collar
- Black Jacket
- Green lightweight army trousers with turn-ups

Travelling with a sketchbook

Sketching as you travel is tremendous fun, very satisfying and a good challenge, since you tend to have to record everything very quickly. However, the subjects of your sketches may not find such enjoyment – they can be curious or resentful, so try to be inconspicuous.

Here are a couple of hints. Keep your equipment to a minimum – things that can fit into a pocket or small bag. Perhaps pretend to be doing something else – I often make out that I am writing postcards.

Despite the heat many people are wrapped up in heavy woollen jellabah with hoods over their heads

Monday 25th August Chaouen Medina

Berber woman wear several heavy layers of clothes including 'long johns'

272

Seasons

Autumn, winter, spring and summer – sometimes it is a positive joy to be working outside; other times this quite plainly is not the case. In the past, I have sketched through a car windscreen as the rain pours or snow falls outside. Keep a camera handy in these instances to capture fleeting effects.

The winter months are a good time to see the landscape stripped bare or simplified by snow. Trees in full leaf frequently obscure interesting architectural details so it is a good time to observe them clearly through the bare branches.

Summer months are good for drawing people at leisure, or strong contrasts of lighting and deep shadow.

Autumn in Britain can usually be relied on to provide some wonderfully misty mornings, perfect for sketching simplified atmospheric perspectives.

Reflections on wet roads or pavements can totally transform a scene and present quite magical subject matter.

Experiments with a variety of media, as in the sketches featured on these pages, will prove their suitability for certain conditions.

Times of day

Apart from climatic changes, the times of day present the artist with a lot of variety and subject matter. Early risers see quiet streets with the milkmen and newspaper deliverers, market traders setting up, joggers, even urban foxes going about their business. Then come commuters heading for the stations, parents taking kids to school, the dog walkers, shoppers and the normal hustle and bustle of town life.

In hot climates you get the midday siesta when people shelter from the sun and only mad dogs and obsessive sketchers go out (sensibly wearing appropriate protection) in search of some visually exciting inspiration.

Twilight or moonlight provide elusive qualities where shapes appear simplified and details disappear. James Whistler captured some of these effects in his 'nocturnes' and wonderful etchings of the river Thames in London.

When it comes to night scenes the American painter Edward Hopper portrayed the city's commonest sights – store windows and lunch counters as an oasis of light in the darkened streets, with people depicted like actors on a stage. Many of his oil paintings were thoroughly planned in a series of on-the-spot tonal crayon sketches, before he put a brush to canvas. For some complex paintings he did as many as thirty or forty such sketches including studies of architectural details and figures.

Light and its effects

The effects of light upon the landscape change throughout the day. At times the light can emphasize particular features of a scene while at other times it can throw the same features into obscurity. These changes can be fleeting and can have a dramatic effect upon the scene, perhaps changing the mood radically. If you are lucky you can return at the same time of day and experience similar conditions, but if this doesn't work, a camera is the only way to capture the mood. However, there are times when only our visual memory or imagination are the ways to fill the gaps.

Wednesday 27th August   Tangier Beach

The Medina

The Kasbah

The docks

Sketching in haste

There is a limit to the amount of detail and information one can include when sketching in a hurry. While this may be a disadvantage at times, it certainly sharpens one's visual shorthand and can produce work which displays great energy and excitement.

To train the hand and eye to sum up essentials, set yourself a time limit per sketch and be sure to move on to a different project.

These sketches were done whilst standing up, using a fibre-tipped pen without any preliminary pencil drawing.

Use of the camera

As we sit and sketch, we are focusing on visual qualities; this can broaden our perceptions so that the whole act becomes a unique, memorable experience. If, for whatever reasons, we have to leave the work unfinished, to continue or develop it elsewhere, a photograph is a good way of recording the information.

If you were sketching a very broad vista which won't fit onto one photograph, take several and stick them together as a panorama or compilation. Try to use your own photos since they represent your own viewpoint, perception and motivation, not those of anyone else.

Close-ups of details or transitory moving elements can all be brought together in a composition. The example shown on this page was compiled from photographs taken during a boat trip down the river Thames.

I have not slavishly copied any particular image but have juggled parts about, altered sizes and left things out. (A more finished sketch from this material appears at the top of page 275.)

There is a value in compiling your own system of reference photographs or magazine cuttings with inspirational images.

Composition

Sketching can be an end in itself or a means of training hand and eye; it can also form a preparation for a composed picture – part of an overall plan to design and organize elements within a defined space. We may use images from a variety of sources – sketchbooks, photographs or magazine cuttings. Basically, images which remind us a of a mood, memory or association rather than images just to copy.

An illustrator working on a commission rarely, if ever, finds subject matter ready-made and has to undertake preliminary studies or show rough visuals to a client before progressing with the finished artwork.

Such preliminary procedures enable alternatives to be evaluated and structures for holding pictorial elements together to be explored. At this stage it is best not to get involved with details. Objects can for the most part be indicated as simple shapes and it becomes a game of fitting them together like a jigsaw pattern. The result should be one of order as averse to confusion.

The sketches on this page show how various alternatives were explored on a small scale to arrive at a more satisfactory arrangement.

The two little girls to the right of the picture were turned round to face inwards and lead the eye to the centre of interest.

When composing a picture we manipulate elements within a design area, adjusting the viewpoint, moving something or even leaving it out. Here are some useful principles.

There is a 'rule of thirds' in every composition, by which imaginary lines divide the picture area into thirds both horizontally and vertically. Strong elements can coincide with these.

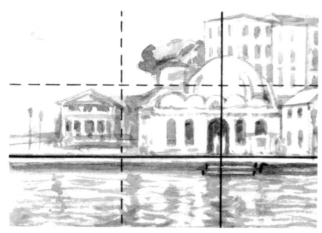

It is well worth making simple thumbnail sketches and exploring and adjusting the arrangement of major forms before starting the final picture.

Simple implied geometrical shapes such as triangles or circles are often the base of a composition. The diagram on the right is based on triangles – look at the basic underlying structure and how key elements are tied to it.

Every picture is based upon the principal of balancing overlapping areas, forms and contours. We define these by drawing them as lines, and so linear arrangement becomes our first consideration.

A main focal point is essential. The eye should be drawn to it by the lines in the picture and lines should cross at the main point of interest.

It can be a very instructive exercise to secure some tracing paper over reproductions or postcards of famous paintings to trace out their basic underlying structures.

The eye should be able to follow a natural path in every good picture, and you can make this happen by clever use of line.

Lead the eye in, give it some interest and then let it pass out of the composition. It should be a pleasing path, free of obstruction or decision. Bring the eye in at the bottom and take it out at the top rather than at the sides. Lines leading out of the subject should be stopped by some device or another line leading back to the focal point.

In the first thumbnail sketch, left, the cars in the centre don't seem sufficiently interesting as the focal point of the composition.

In the final composition, below, a couple of seated figures add human interest. The timber-framed building on the right helps redirect the eye back towards the centre of interest.

Exploring alternatives with market stalls and shoppers.

Locating figures

People add interest to paintings, providing a sort of empathy that enables us in some way to enter the picture. This fact grants a certain power to any figures included.

All the elements of a good composition should fit well together. Take a look at the work of many past and contemporary painters and you can see how much attention has gone into their composition. A good way of studying this is to lay a piece of tracing paper over a postcard or reproduction, and then trace the major sub-divisions and lines of sight which the artist has used. You will see how carefully and effectively he or she has placed each figure, animal, group or object.

This does not mean to say that figures should be sharply defined; often a strategically placed blob of paint, a shape or flick of colour will suffice. This is most appropriate when the rest of the painting is equally simplified.

However, with more detailed paintings other factors, such as perspective, gesture and shape, must be considered. It must be apparent what the figures are doing, what clothes they are wearing, how old they are, if they are male or female, what their relationship is to each other. This is when keeping, and constantly using, a sketchbook is particularly vital since many of these details are hard to record without practised observation and experience.

The above illustration was for a magazine and had to include certain elements to create an impression of a particular place.

To get your figures to hang on the horizon line, make the line cut through the figures in the same place. Notice how some figures have been incorporated in the composition opposite.

Building a composition

This final example demonstrates a compilation from sketches and photographs being brought together in a pictorial composition.

You can write on your sketches to remind yourself of important features or make notes about the possible use of colour, perhaps.

The sketches on this page are my thumbnail layouts of human interest for the final composition on page 285.

Conclusion

I hope that having read this book you are encouraged to go out and buy some basic materials and get sketching. You will soon find out what a tremendous pleasure it is. There is no need to be daunted, especially if you remember the following points.

• Consider your sketchbooks to be private and personal, your way of expressing yourself without inhibition.

• It is cheap and easy to get equipped for sketching.

• Sketchbooks can be big or small; choose either to suit your personality.

• The best subject matter can be very close to home so you needn't necessarily search far afield.

• Keep trying and you will soon get to grips with perspective.

• Start off with simple tones and shapes and then move on to details.

• Practise sketching at speed since it hones your visual shorthand skills.

• What you put in your sketchbook when you are travelling will be a permanent and personal reminder of your experiences.

• Use your sketchbook as a reference book containing your draft sketches, thumbnail layouts and trial compositions.

• Remember to lead the eye to a major focal point and to include people so that the viewer is able to empathize with the picture.

• As well as your sketches, a variety of other visual sources can be useful in compiling a picture. Try making a collection of photographs, postcards and written notes on colour which can later be brought into play in a studio situation.